Eric L. Einspruch
RMC Research Corporation

Next Steps
With SPSS®

W0006738

CW00921445

SAGE Publications
International Educational and Professional Publisher
Thousand Oaks ■ London ■ New Delhi

For information:

 Sage Publications, Inc.
2455 Teller Road
Thousand Oaks, California 91320
E-mail: order@sagepub.com

Sage Publications Ltd.
6 Bonhill Street
London EC2A 4PU
United Kingdom

Sage Publications India Pvt. Ltd.
B-42, Panchsheel Enclave
Post Box 4109
New Delhi 110 017 India

Printed in the United States of America

Library of Congress Cataloging-in-Publication Data

Einspruch, Eric L.
Next steps with SPSS / Eric L. Einspruch.
    p. cm.
Includes bibliographical references and index.
ISBN 0–7619–1963–5 (cloth)—ISBN 0–7619–1964–3 (pbk.)
    1. SPSS (Computer file) 2. Social sciences-Statistical methods-Computer programs. I. Title.
HA32.E448 2004
300.´285´5369—dc21

                                        2003000683

03   04   05   06   10   9   8   7   6   5   4   3   2   1

Acquisitions Editors:	C. Deborah Laughton and Alison Mudditt
Editorial Assistants:	Veronica K. Novak and Alicia Carter
Production Editor:	Melanie Birdsall
Copy Editor:	Connie Adams
Typesetter:	C&M Digitals (P) Ltd.
Proofreader:	Cheryl Rivard
Cover Designer:	Michelle Lee

Contents

Acknowledgments

I owe a debt of gratitude to many people who have directly or indirectly contributed to this book. C. Deborah Laughton, my editor at Sage Publications, Inc., was instrumental in bringing the book to fruition. Authors granted me permission to quote examples from their work. Reviewers of drafts of the manuscript provided helpful insights and suggestions. SPSS, Inc., was accessible and provided me with information about updates to their software. Thank you to each of you.

I would also like to express my sincere appreciation to the many family members, friends, colleagues, and students who have encouraged and supported my interest in research and statistics and who have taught me much over the years. I am ever grateful to you.

CHAPTER 1

Introduction

Data collection, analysis, interpretation, and reporting are critically important in many areas today. This is true whether one is learning about customer satisfaction, evaluating a program, or gathering information for decision making. The Statistical Package for the Social Sciences (SPSS) program is a powerful data analysis tool with many exciting features available to those who wish to advance beyond the novice level. The purpose of this book is to open doors that will allow you to enter the world of intermediate and advanced SPSS skills. These skills are introduced and illustrated with sample programs designed to apply powerful techniques in data handling and analysis. The output from the programs is presented and interpreted. Chapter exercises are provided and their solutions may be found in the Appendix. Once you have a basic understanding of these skills, you will be well on your way to becoming a strong SPSS user.

This book meets the need for an introduction to intermediate- and advanced-level skills for students and practitioners who have mastered the fundamentals of SPSS and who now need to enhance their SPSS skills. It provides a means for readers to achieve a working knowledge of the more advanced features of using SPSS that are not covered in an introductory guide. These features should be considered a collection of tools rather than merely "tricks of the trade." Once familiar with the availability of these tools, readers will want to expand their understanding by applying these tools to their own data analytic tasks.

This book serves students and professionals who have completed one or two statistics courses, who have learned the basics of SPSS, and who now need a more thorough understanding of the power of SPSS. Specifically, readers who are able to perform the following tasks will be prepared to use this text:

- Create SPSS data sets, define data files (including missing data), code data, and enter data.

- Read SPSS and ASCII data sets.

- Run SPSS and navigate its various windows, including the Data Editor, Syntax Editor, and Output Viewer.

- Recode data, compute data values, and select cases from a data set.

- Merge data sets (adding cases and adding variables).

- Use SPSS pull-down menus to perform statistical analyses.

- Write, debug, and run SPSS syntax to perform the various SPSS tasks listed above.

Readers who do not yet possess these skills will benefit from first developing them using an introductory book (for example, see Einspruch, 1998). Readers who are quite comfortable with these skills and who have gained proficiency at writing SPSS syntax will be well prepared to understand the material in this book. Readers who are familiar with handling complex data files, looping functions, macros, pivot tables, interactive graphics, the production facility, and scripting likely will have already advanced beyond the scope of this book.

This book also assumes that readers are comfortable working with SPSS using both pull-down menus and syntax code and are comfortable alternating between the two approaches. The material in this book draws from both approaches: The chapters on handling complex data files, looping functions, and macros involve considerable use of the syntax code (and scripting involves use of similar code), and the chapters on pivot tables, interactive graphics, and the production facility rely on pull-down windows. The reason for this alternating approach is that some of SPSS's many powerful features are accessed through coding and others are accessed through pull-down windows. Thus, the strong user understands how to access a needed feature and is flexible in moving between the two approaches.

Readers should also be aware that this book introduces features that might be thought of as their own "language." In particular, the chapter on macros introduces a way of thinking about SPSS syntax code beyond its basic use. The chapter on scripting introduces a way of working with SPSS that is qualitatively different than the syntax language, and the chapter on the matrix command language expands SPSS syntax in a manner similar to that of macros. Readers need at least a modest level of experience writing syntax code before attempting the material in these chapters.

This book is organized so that it begins by building increasingly advanced syntax coding skills, beginning with handling complex data files and then developing looping and macro skills. The book then switches to more windows-oriented skills that are suited for working with SPSS output (i.e., the chapters on pivot tables and interactive graphics) and for running SPSS in an alternative mode (i.e., the chapter on the production facility). Finally, the book returns to coding skills, introducing the more advanced topics of the scripting facility (which has broad application to handling data and creating output) and the matrix command language.

Beyond this introduction, Chapter 2 covers topics related to *working with data files*. The chapter focuses on managing both simple and complex data files and covers features that can be applied to data sets to make them easier to use or to solve challenges. In addition, the chapter covers reading and managing complex data files (i.e., files that are not rectangular in structure).

Chapter 3 examines *looping functions*. These functions can be used to repeatedly perform a set of commands. When the command needs to be performed only a small number of times, then it may be easier to do so directly. However, a looped structure is a far more efficient coding scheme if the command needs to be performed a large number of times (potentially saving tens, hundreds, or thousands of lines of code). In addition, errors may be avoided by limiting the amount of code that is written.

Chapter 4 explores the SPSS *macro facility*. A macro is a set of commands that can be used to reduce the time and effort needed to perform complex and repetitive tasks. For example, macros can be used to repeatedly issue a series of commands using looping functions or to produce output from several procedures using a single command. Thus, macros represent a powerful command syntax feature within SPSS.

Chapter 5 covers working with *pivot tables*. Many SPSS procedures produce results that appear in the Viewer as pivot tables that display information in rows, columns, and layers that can be exchanged (i.e., a row can be made a column and a column can be made a row). The Pivot Table Editor can also be used to modify pivot tables.

Chapter 6 looks at the SPSS *interactive graphics feature*. Interactive charts can be created and maintained dynamically. Once a chart is created, its appearance or the roles of variables in the chart can be modified, and the changes will appear in the Output Viewer as soon as they are made (rather than having to wait for a procedure to be rerun). Changes can be made until the chart provides the illustration that best reveals the data.

Chapter 7 addresses the SPSS *production facility.* The production facility allows users to run SPSS programs unattended so the user can do other things while SPSS is running. The user writes a program or a set of programs that are then run by the production facility. This feature can be used to run routine, time-consuming analyses.

Chapter 8 introduces the SPSS *scripting facility,* which may be used to automate SPSS tasks. The scripting facility is a powerful tool for working with many elements of the SPSS software.

Chapter 9 introduces the SPSS *matrix command language.* The matrix command language is used to perform mathematical calculations using matrix algebra. It allows users to write their own statistical routines using matrix algebra. Matrix command language skills are important for many who use advanced statistical techniques.

This book takes a straightforward approach to what readers need to know to advance their SPSS skills beyond the novice level. Hence its title, *Next Steps With SPSS.* It is especially appropriate for readers who have mastered the basics of SPSS and who are now in need of more fully understanding the power available to them in SPSS but who wish to be guided in this exploration in a more friendly manner than that which is typically taken in the software manuals. The book has been written in an easy-to-read manner that takes the reader step-by-step through detailed examples. For each major topic, the book focuses on the key ideas within the topic rather than getting bogged down in the details of the many available options.

I encourage you to enter and run the programs as you work with this book to develop a practical mastery of the skills. I also recommend that you keep in mind that the SPSS manuals are your friends and that you consult them often, for they contain a wealth of information beyond the scope of this book. Readers who require additional information beyond what is covered in this book will have gained a great enough understanding that they can effectively use the SPSS manuals as reference tools. But most important, I encourage you to have fun as you look into the vast realm of powerful tools that SPSS has to offer.

CHAPTER 2

Working With Data Files

Chapter Purpose

This chapter introduces SPSS syntax that can be used to label files and data, manipulate data, read complex data files, and clear data files.

Chapter Goal

To enhance readers' knowledge of SPSS's capabilities for reading and managing data.

Expectation of Readers

Readers will be able to make the most use of this chapter if they are comfortable writing and running SPSS syntax and have a basic understanding of data handling operations. Readers are expected to write and run the SPSS code that is presented in the chapter so that they see the result of the operations.

INTRODUCTION

This chapter focuses on managing both simple and complex data files. An example data set is first presented. This data set is then used to illustrate techniques of labeling data, manipulating data, and reading complex data files. You will find this chapter easiest to understand if you create the data set in SPSS and use it to try out the techniques as they are discussed. Begin by entering only the first 10 records and providing variable and value labels. Then save the 10-record data set as 'Wintergreen1.sav.'

Lewis-Beck (1995) presented a hypothetical data set of results from a study of influences on *academic ability.* In his example, the Academic Affairs Office of Wintergreen College commissioned a study to investigate the determinants of success on a first-year entrance examination. A sample of 50 first-year students was drawn from a list of all 500 first-year students provided by the registrar, and each student in the sample was assigned a unique *respondent number.* Student scores were obtained on a 100-item entrance examination of *academic ability* (scores were simply the number of items correct on the examination). In addition, a 36-item survey was administered to students in face-to-face interviews. This survey provided information on several key variables, including *parents' education* (the average number of years of schooling for each parent), *student motivation* (based on the response to a question about whether or not the student would be willing to spend extra hours studying), *religion* (Catholic, Protestant, or Jewish), *gender* (male or female), and the *community type* from which the student came (urban or rural). Finally, students' admissions materials were available, including the academic advisor's handwritten comments assessing each student's likelihood to succeed in college. These comments were grouped into a variable called *advisor evaluation* (with the categories of "likely to succeed," "could succeed or could fail," and "likely to fail"). The codebook for this study is presented in Figure 2.1 and the data are presented in Figure 2.2.

LABELING FILES AND DATA

Files, data, and output are easiest to read if they are well documented. Good documentation also helps the user remember the contents of the file and data when they are set aside for a period of time before returning to them. It also helps the user remain familiar with data sets when working on different projects at the same time. SPSS offers several methods for documenting files. SPSS also provides ways to reveal the file documentation. In addition, you can add labels to values of variables without removing existing values, and you can apply the data dictionary from one data set to another. We explore each of these topics in this section.

Chapter Glossary

Add files: An SPSS command used to combine files when each file contributes additional cases with the same variables.

Add value labels: An SPSS command that adds or modifies value labels for a variable without affecting the labels of other values of that variable.

Apply dictionary: An SPSS command that uses one data file to supply variable and value information to another data file.

Autorecode: An SPSS command that recodes the values of variables into consecutive integers and assigns the recoded values to a new variable.

Count: An SPSS command used to count, for each case, the number of times a particular value (or range of values) occurs across a set of variables.

Display: An SPSS command that provides information about the working data file.

Document: An SPSS command that allows text to be saved in an SPSS data file.

Drop document: An SPSS command that removes documentation from an SPSS data file.

Erase: An SPSS command that erases a specified file from the disk. *Use with caution!*

File label: An SPSS command that provides a descriptive label for a data file.

Grouped data files: Data files in which each case is spread across multiple records (e.g., case 1, records 1 through 3; case 2, records 1 through 3; etc.).

Match files: An SPSS command used to combine files when each file contributes additional variables to the same cases.

N of cases: An SPSS command that limits the number of cases in the working data file to a specified number.

Nested data files: Data files that contain more than one type of record and in which all records of one type follow records of another type (e.g., class 1, students 1 through 10; class 2, students 11 through 20; etc.).

New file: An SPSS command that clears the working data file.

Numeric: An SPSS command that creates a new numeric variable that is added to the working data file.

Sample: An SPSS command used to draw a random sample of cases from the working data file.

Split file: An SPSS command that divides the working data file into subgroups that are then analyzed separately.

String: An SPSS command that creates a new string variable that is added to the working data file.

Sysfile info: An SPSS command that provides information about a data file that is not the working data file.

Update: An SPSS command used to update information in one file with information from another file or files.

Variable name:	AA
Variable label:	Academic Ability
Values:	Number of items correct on 100-item entrance examination
Variable name:	PE
Variable label:	Parents' Education
Values:	Average years of education for mother and father
Variable name:	SM
Variable label:	Student Motivation
Values and value labels:	0 Not willing
	1 Undecided
	2 Willing
Variable name:	AE
Variable label:	Advisor Evaluation
Values and value labels:	0 Fail
	1 Succeed or fail
	2 Succeed
Variable name:	R
Variable label:	Religious Affiliation
Values and value labels:	0 Catholic
	1 Protestant
	2 Jewish
Variable name:	G
Variable label:	Gender
Values and value labels:	0 Male
	1 Female
Variable name:	C
Variable label:	Community Type
Values and value labels:	0 Urban
	1 Rural

Figure 2.1   Codebook for the Wintergreen Study

Respondent Number	AA	PE	SM	AE	R	G	C
01	93	19	1	2	0	0	1
02	46	12	0	0	0	0	0
03	57	15	1	1	0	0	0
04	94	18	2	2	1	1	1
05	82	13	2	1	1	1	1
06	59	12	0	0	2	0	0
07	61	12	1	2	0	0	0
08	29	9	0	0	1	1	0
09	36	13	1	1	0	0	0
10	91	16	2	2	1	1	0
11	55	10	0	0	1	0	0
12	58	11	0	1	0	0	0
13	67	14	1	1	0	1	1
14	77	14	1	2	2	1	0
15	71	12	0	0	2	1	0
16	83	16	2	2	1	0	1
17	96	15	2	2	2	0	1
18	87	12	1	1	0	0	1
19	62	11	0	0	0	0	0
20	52	9	0	1	2	1	0
21	46	10	1	0	0	1	0
22	91	20	2	2	1	0	0
23	85	17	2	1	1	1	1
24	48	11	1	1	2	0	0
25	81	17	1	1	1	1	1
26	74	16	2	1	2	1	0
27	68	12	2	1	1	1	1
28	63	12	1	0	0	0	1
29	72	14	0	2	0	0	0
30	99	19	1	1	1	0	0
31	64	13	1	1	0	0	0
32	77	13	1	0	1	1	1
33	88	16	2	2	0	1	0

Figure 2.2 Data for the Wintergreen Study

Respondent Number	AA	PE	SM	AE	R	G	C
34	54	09	0	1	1	0	0
35	86	17	1	2	1	0	1
36	73	15	1	1	0	1	0
37	79	15	2	1	0	0	1
38	85	14	2	1	2	1	1
39	96	16	0	1	1	0	1
40	59	12	1	0	0	1	0
41	84	14	1	0	1	0	1
42	71	15	2	1	1	0	0
43	89	15	0	1	0	1	1
44	38	12	1	0	1	1	0
45	62	11	1	1	2	0	1
46	93	16	1	0	1	0	1
47	71	13	2	1	1	0	0
48	55	11	0	1	0	0	0
49	74	15	1	2	0	1	0
50	88	18	1	1	0	1	0

Figure 2.2 Data for the Wintergreen Study (continued)

File Label

The file label command provides a descriptive label for a data file, which is then added to the data dictionary and is displayed in the Notes section of the SPSS output (or on the first line of each page of SPSS draft output). Let's start by reading the data file as is and listing its contents. Enter and run the following syntax code in the SPSS Syntax window (be sure you specify the complete path that points to the location of your data set; also, do not enter the numbers at the beginning of the line— e.g., "1)"—as they appear simply for reference in this book):

```
1) *
2) * This code reads the Wintergreen1 data set and lists
```

```
 3) * the cases in the data set
 4) * Remember, everything between the first asterisk and
 5) * the next period in this code is considered a
 6) * "comment" and is ignored by SPSS
 7) * The use of multiple asterisks is simply stylistic
 8) *.
 9) get file = '/pathname/wintergreen1.sav.'
10) list cases.
```

Look at the Notes section of the SPSS output and you will see that a file label does not appear. Now write and run the following code to label the Wintergreen data set:

```
1) *
2) * This code reads the Wintergreen1 data set, assigns
3) * a label to the data file, and lists
4) * the cases in the data set
5) *.
6) get file = '/pathname/wintergreen1.sav.'
7) file label Wintergreen academic ability study (Lewis-Beck).
8) list cases.
```

Again, look at the Notes section of the SPSS output. Now you will see that a file label appears and that it contains the text you entered in your syntax code. You have now added your first bit of documentation to the data file. This documentation can be invaluable in helping you keep track of information about the data set.

Document and Drop Document

You can use the document command to save any amount of text in an SPSS data file. This text can be displayed using the display command (see below). A period at the end of the text terminates the command so should only be used at the end of the text. The document command is only available through the Syntax window. To add documentation to the Wintergreen data set, write and run the following code (notice that although the documentation is assigned, this syntax does not cause it to be displayed):

```
1) *
2) * This code reads the Wintergreen1 data set, assigns
3) * documentation to the data file, and lists
4) * the cases in the data set
5) *.
6) get file = '/pathname/wintergreen1.sav.'
7) document Hypothetical data set of results from a
8) study of influences on academic ability
9)    presented by Lewis-Beck (1995) commissioned by
10)   the Academic Affairs Office of Wintergreen
11)   College to investigate the determinants of
12)   success on a first-year entrance examination.
13)   list cases.
```

You can use multiple document commands to add additional text to the documentation. You can also use the drop documents command to remove the documentation from the working data file.

Display

The display command provides information from the working data file. This command is available only from the Syntax window. The most complete information about the file is returned by the last two lines of the following code (display requires one line of code for each keyword):

```
1) *
2) * This code reads the Wintergreen1 data set and
3) * displays both the documentation for the data
4) * set and the data dictionary
5) *.
6) get file = '/pathname/wintergreen1.sav.'
7) display documents.
8) display dictionary.
```

Notice that the SPSS output now contains File Information that displays the data file documentation and the data dictionary. The first command (display documents) provides information about the file documentation. The second command (display dictionary) provides complete information from the dictionary of the working data file, including variable names, labels, sequential position in the file, print and write formats, missing values, and value labels. The display command can show the variables sorted alphabetically by coding it as

```
1) display sorted dictionary.
```

The display command is useful for exploring the contents of a data file, especially if it is either being encountered for the first time or after a long period of time. If you have entered the Wintergreen data along with labels and documentation and made it your working data file, the output from these two commands appears as shown in Figure 2.3.

Sysfile Info

O The sysfile info command returns information about the file itself (including the file label but not the documentation) as well as the same variable information as the display dictionary command. The difference between the sysfile info and display commands is that you use sysfile info to find out information about a file that is not the working data file and you use display to find out information about a file that is the working data file. To see how the sysfile info command works, clear the working data file and then write the following code in the Syntax window (be sure to include any necessary additional path specifications to point to your file):

O Go to the Data Editor window.

O From the pull-down menus, select **File, New, Data.**

```
1) *
2) * This code returns information about the
3) * Wintergreen1 data set, which is not
4) * currently the working data file
5) *.
6) sysfile info file = 'Wintergreen1.sav.'
```

```
display documents.
```

File Information

```
document Hypothetical data set of results from a
study of influences on academic ability presented
by Lewis-Beck (1995) Commissioned by the Academic
Affairs Wintergreen College to investigate the
determinants of success on a first year entrance
exam.
```

```
display dictionary.
```

File Information

```
        List of variables on the working file
```

Name		Position
RESP_NUM	Respondent Number Measurement Level: Scale Column Width: 8 Alignment: Right Print Format: F8.2 Write Format: F8.2	1
AA	Academic Ability Measurement Level: Scale Column Width: 8 Alignment: Right Print Format: F8.2 Write Format: F8.2	2
PE	Parents' Education Measurement Level: Scale Column Width: 8 Alignment: Right Print Format: F8.2 Write Format: F8.2	3
SM	Student Motivation Measurement Level: Scale Column Width: 8 Alignment: Right Print Format: F8.2 Write Format: F8.2	4

Figure 2.3 Output From Display Command

Name		Position
Value	*Label*	
.00	Not willing	
1.00	Undecided	
2.00	Willing	

AE   Advisor Evaluation   5
          Measurement Level: Scale
          Column Width: 8 Alignment: Right
          Print Format: F8.2
          Write Format: F8.2

Value	*Label*
.00	Fail
1.00	Succeed or fail
2.00	Succeed

R   Religious Affiliation   6
          Measurement Level: Scale
          Column Width: 8 Alignment: Right
          Print Format: F8.2
          Write Format: F8.2

Value	*Label*
.00	Catholic
1.00	Protestant
2.00	Jewish

G   Gender   7
          Measurement Level: Scale
          Column Width: 8 Alignment: Right
          Print Format: F8.2
          Write Format: F8.2

Value	*Label*
.00	Male
1.00	Female

C   Community Type   8
          Measurement Level: Scale
          Column Width: 8 Alignment:
          Right
          Print Format: F8.2
          Write Format: F8.2

Value	*Label*
.00	Urban
1.00	Rural

Figure 2.3 Output From Display Command (continued)

Finally, run the code and view the result in the Output Viewer window. You will see that a considerable amount of information about the file has been displayed.

Add Value Labels

Sometimes it is necessary to add or modify the value labels for a variable. The command add value labels allows you to add or modify value labels for a variable without affecting the labels of the other values. For example, suppose that at the time the 'Wintergreen1.sav' data set was created you knew that the variable "c" should be labeled "community type" and that the value 0 should be labeled "urban" but you did not know the label for the value 1 (perhaps you did not recall whether it was "nonurban" or "rural"). After confirming at a later time that the label should indeed be "rural," from the Syntax window, you would write and run the following code (this command is available only through SPSS Syntax):

```
1) *
2) * This code returns information about the
3) * Wintergreen1 data set, which is not
4) * currently the working data file
5) *.
6) add value labels c 1 'Rural.'
```

Similar rules apply as for the value labels command. However, if you were to run value labels, you would delete other existing value labels (e.g., "Urban" for the value 0 in this example). This could be a significant inconvenience if you are working with a variable with many values.

You can also perform this labeling task via the "Variable View" tab in the Data Editor window. This provides you with a second method of accomplishing the task (one syntax based and one windows based). Neither one is right or wrong, but one or the other may be preferred in a particular circumstance. The important thing is to be skilled in both approaches so that you can use the one you feel best with in a given situation.

Apply Dictionary

The command apply dictionary allows you to use one SPSS data file to supply variable and value information to another SPSS data file. The file containing the dictionary information is called the *source file* and the file to which the dictionary information is being applied is called the *target file*. The target file must be the working data file (i.e., you must have the target file open in SPSS). The variables in the source and target files must have the same name and type (i.e., numeric, string, etc.) for the information to be applied. Variables that do not have matching names and types are not changed in the target file. The data dictionary can be used to apply variable labels, value labels, missing value specifications, print and write formats for numeric variables, and weighting information. The data dictionary does not add or remove variables. Also, it treats all value labels as a set (i.e., for a given matching variable, all value labels are applied). The same is true for missing value specifications.

The see how `apply dictionary` works, open a new data file as follows:

○ Open the Data Editor window.

○ From the pull-down menus, select **File, New, Data.**

Now enter the second 10 records from the wintergreen data but do not give them any variable or value labels. Give the variables the same names as those in Wintergreen1.sav. Save the new data in a file called 'Wintergreen2.sav.' Complete the following steps to apply the data dictionary:

○ Open the Data Editor window.

○ From the pull-down menus, select **File, Apply Data Dictionary . . . .**

○ When the "Apply SPSS Dictionary" dialog box appears (see Figure 2.4), choose Wintergreen1.sav (either double-click the file name or single-click the file name and then click the "Open" button).

Notice that the working data file (Wintergreen2.sav) now contains all the labeling information that is contained in Wintergreen1.sav. Imagine the amount of time this can save when you create files with unique data but similar variables.

To perform this skill from the Syntax window, write and run the following code (be sure to include any necessary additional path specifications to point to your files):

```
1) *
2) * This code applies the data dictionary from the
3) * file with the first 10 Wintergreen cases to
4) * the file with the second 10
```

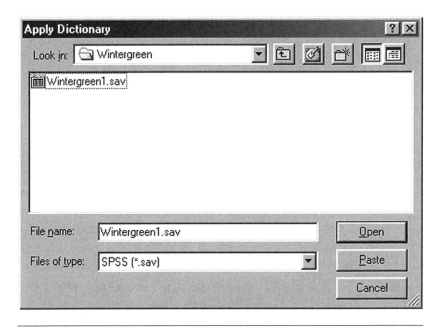

Figure 2.4

```
5) * Wintergreen cases
6) *.
7) get file = 'Wintergreen2.sav.'
8) apply dictionary from 'Wintergreen1.sav.'
```

MANIPULATING DATA

This section covers several skills related to data manipulation. We will look at options that are available when you add or match files, automatically recoding data into consecutive integers and counting occurrences of a value. We will also examine how to limit the number of cases that are read from a data set. We will see how to create new numeric and string variables, how to draw a sample of cases from a data file, how to split the file for analysis by subgroup, and how to update files.

Add Files (and Match Files)

The add files command is used to combine from 2 to 50 files when each file contributes additional cases with the same variables. For example, you could use the add files command to combine the two Wintergreen data sets that you have entered so far (Wintergreen1.sav and Wintergreen2.sav) into a single data set with 20 cases, all of which have the same variables. This command has several features, a few of which are highlighted here. If the files have the same variables but those variables have been given different names in each of the files, you can use the rename keyword to assign common names to the variables (it is not unusual for similar variables in different files to have different names if the data entry process was not set up in advance to avoid this situation). You can also use the in keyword to create a new variable that indicates the file from which the cases came. This is particularly handy when you want to identify those particular records for either data cleaning or data analysis purposes. Finally, you can use the keep keyword to list the variables you wish to retain in the final data set. Alternatively, you can use the drop keyword to list the variables you do not wish to keep. The choice whether to use keep or drop depends mainly on your style of writing SPSS syntax code. Similar features are available for the match files command, which is used to combine files with the same cases but different variables.

To see how these features function, first enter cases 21 through 30 from the Wintergreen data set into the Data Editor window. However, give the variables the following names: Name the variable for respondent number "rn," the variable for academic ability "acad," the variable for parent education "par_ed," the variable for student motivation "motivate," the variable for advisor evaluation "ad_eval," the variable for religious affiliation "religion," the variable for gender "gender," and the variable for community type "ct." Also add an additional variable called "new_var" and assign it any values you wish. Finally, save the data set as a file named 'Wintergreen3.sav.'

Now write and run the following SPSS code (be sure to include any necessary additional path specifications to point to your files):

```
1) *
2) * This code illustrates three features of the "add
3) * files" command
4) * "in ="
5) * "rename ="
6) * "drop ="
7) *.
8) add files file = 'c:\Wintergreen1.sav'/
```

```
 9)    in = w1/
10)    file = 'c:\Wintergreen2.sav'/
11)    in = w2/
12)    file = 'Wintergreen3.sav'/
13)    rename = (rn, acad, par_ed, motivate,
14)    ad_eval, religion, gender, ct =
15)    resp_num, aa, pe, sm, ae, r, g, c)/
16)    in = w3/
17)    drop = new_var.
18) execute.
```

Let's take a look at each line of this code. Lines 1–7 provide comments for the code. Line 8 starts the SPSS add files command and reads the data from the first Wintergreen file. Line 9 creates a new variable, named "w1," which contains the value 1 for all cases read from the first Wintergreen file and the value 0 for all cases read from the remaining files. Line 10 reads (and appends) the data from the second Wintergreen file, and line 11 creates a new variable, named "w2," which contains the value 1 for all cases read from the second Wintergreen file and the value 0 for all cases read from the other files. Line 12 reads (and appends) the data from the third Wintergreen file. Lines 13–15 are included because the variables in the third Wintergreen file do not have the same names as those in the first two files, even though they are indeed the same variables. These lines rename the variables in the third Wintergreen file to match the names in the first two files. Line 16 creates a new variable, named "w3," which contains the value 1 for all cases read from the third Wintergreen file and the value 0 for all cases read from the other files. Line 17 drops the variable named "new_var" from the third Wintergreen file as it is read into the combined data set. Line 18 causes the program to be run.

Examine your resulting data set to see that the working data file has 30 cases (10 from each of the data files) and that all the variables have the same name so that all the cases have data for those variables. Also confirm that there are three new variables, "w1," "w2," and "w3." As noted above, the variable "w1" has a value of 1 for the 10 cases from the Wintergreen1.sav data file and the value 0 for cases from the other two data files. The variables "w2" and "w3" contain values that have been similarly assigned. The variable "new_var" is not included in the data set.

Autorecode

The autorecode command recodes the values of variables into consecutive integers and assigns the recoded values to a new variable. Autorecode works similarly to the recode command except that autorecode automatically assigns the new values and recode requires that you assign the new values. Autorecode gives the original variable and value labels to the new variable.

Autorecode is a useful command for three different situations. First, because SPSS Tables truncates long string variables but not their labels, you can use autorecode to give a long string variable numeric values that have the original long strings as the value labels. This allows more complete text to be displayed in the table.

Second, if a categorical variable has values that are nonconsecutive integers, you can use autorecode to assign them as consecutive integers (e.g., consider a study in which subjects are given one of three different doses of a treatment, either 5, 10, or 20 units; autorecode would recode these values as 1, 2, and 3). This allows SPSS to be more efficient in processing the data.

Third, autorecode can convert a string variable into a numeric one (e.g., a variable called "gender" with values of f for female and m for male could be autorecoded into a variable with values of 1 for female and 2 for male). This is important because many of SPSS's analytic commands require that categorical variables be numeric (e.g., the ANOVA command).

Before looking at the autorecode command, let's recall that the recode command requires that you designate the new values being assigned to the variable. For example, you could use the following line of syntax if you want to create a new variable called "ngender" (for "new" gender) and assign to it the values contained in the variable "g" but code them as 1 (rather than f) for female and 2 (rather than m) for male:

```
1)  recode g ("f" = 1) ("m" = 2) into ngender.
```

To see how the autorecode command works, enter cases number 31 through 40 from the Wintergreen data, but for the values of the variable "gender," enter f for female and m for male. Save the file as 'Wintergreen4.sav.' Then write and run the following code:

```
1)  *
2)  * This code illustrates the use of the autorecode
3)  * command
4)  *.
5)  get file = 'Wintergreen4.sav.'
6)  autorecode gender into rgender.
```

Examine the working data set to see that the new variable "rgender" (for "recoded gender") has been created, that it has the same variable label as the original variable, and that it has the values of 1 for female and 2 for male.

Count

The count command is used to count, for each case, the number of times a particular value (or range of values) occurs across a set of variables. For example, suppose that students are given a survey at the end of their first year at Wintergreen College asking them about their level of satisfaction with the college experience. The survey contains 10 items (numbered Item01 to Item10), and students rate each item on a scale of 1 to 5. To count the number of times students rated an item as a 1, you would write the following syntax code:

```
1)  count number = Item01 to Item10 (1).
```

The count command creates a new variable (called "number" in this example) that contains the count for each case of an occurrence of the rating 1 across the 10 items. In this example, the variable "number" can take values ranging from 0 (i.e., no items rated 1) to 10 (i.e., all items rated 1). To count the number of items that were rated 3, 4, or 5, you would write the following code:

```
1)  count number = Item01 to Item10 (3 thru 5).
```

Note that the count command ignores user-defined missing values and counts those values as if they were not missing.

N of Cases

The n of cases command limits the number of cases in the working data file to a specified number. For example, to open the Wintergreen1.sav data file and limit the file to the first five cases, write the following code:

```
1) *
2) * This code illustrates the use of the n of cases
3) * command
4) *.
5) get file = 'Wintergreen1.sav.'
6) list cases.
7) n of cases 5.
8) list cases.
```

Lines 1–4 provide comments for this code. Line 5 reads the first Wintergreen data file, and line 6 lists the cases. Line 7 of the code limits further analysis to the first five cases, and line 8 lists the cases once more. If you run this syntax and examine the output, you will notice that all cases appear the first time the list cases command is run but only the first five cases appear the second time the list cases command is run.

The n of cases command is especially useful when you have large data sets and are writing and debugging code that conducts time-consuming data processing or analyses. By limiting the number of cases with which you are working (e.g., to 100 cases), you limit the amount of time it takes each time you run your program. Once you have discovered and corrected all your coding mistakes, you can run the program on the entire data set. *Be careful not to save your data set with the restricted number of cases or all cases beyond the specified number will be lost and you will have to reenter them (or retrieve them from your backup file if you have one).*

Numeric

The numeric command creates a new numeric variable that is added to the working data file. The command is simply written as

```
1) numeric new_var.
```

In this example, the new variable called "new_var" is created. You can also create more than one new variable at a time as

```
1) numeric new_var1 to new_var5.
```

In this example, five new variables are created: "new_var1," "new_var2," "new_var3," "new_var4," and "new_var5." Once created, the numeric variable can be assigned values using commands such as compute, if, recode, and count. To see how this function works, write and run the following syntax code:

```
1) *
2) * This code illustrates the use of the numeric
3) * command
4) *.
5) get file = 'Wintergreen1.sav.'
6) numeric new_var.
7) compute new_var = aa/2.
8) execute.
```

Lines 1–4 provide comments for this code. Line 5 of this syntax reads the first Wintergreen file. Line 6 creates a new numeric variable named "new_var," and line 7 assigns a value to "new_var" that is half the value of the variable for academic ability ("aa"). Line 8 of the code causes the data transformation (i.e., creating the new variable and computing its value) to occur. Look at your data set in the Data Editor window to confirm that the variable "new_var" has been created and that is has the correct value.

In general, the execute command can be used anywhere in your syntax that you want SPSS to run the syntax you have given it. However, each time you execute the commands, the computer passes through your data set to follow the instructions you gave it. The amount of time this takes is trivial when the data set is small but can be quite substantial if the data set is large. Thus, you will use your computing time most efficiently if you minimize the number of times the computer passes through your data set. The execute command is implied when you run an analysis procedure (e.g., frequencies).

String

The "string" command creates a new string variable that is added to the working data file. The command is simply written as

```
1) string new_str (a2).
```

In this example, the new variable called "new_str" is created and has a string format two characters wide. You can create a string of different length by specifying a different number in parentheses; for example, "(a10)" creates a string that is 10 characters wide. You can also create more than one new variable at a time with code such as

```
1) string new_str1 to new_ str5 (a2).
```

In this example, five new variables are created: "new_str1," "new_str2," "new_str3," "new_str4," and "new_str5." Once created, the string variables can be assigned values using commands such as compute, if, recode, and count. To see how this function works, write and run the following syntax code:

```
1) *
2) This code illustrates the use of the string
3) command
4) *.
5) get file = 'Wintergreen1.sav.'
6) string new_str (a2).
7) compute new_str = "zz."
8) execute.
```

Lines 1–4 provide comments for this code. Line 5 of this syntax reads the first Wintergreen file. Line 6 creates a new numeric variable named "new_str," and line 7 assigns "new_str" the value zz. Line 8 of the code causes the data transformation (i.e., creating the new variable and computing its value) to occur. Look at your data set in the Data Editor window to confirm that the variable "new_str" has been created and that it has the correct value.

Sample

The `sample` command is used to draw a random sample of cases from the working data file. You can either specify a proportion of cases for the sample or an exact number of cases. If you specify a proportion of cases for the sample, SPSS usually draws an approximate rather than an exact proportion. For example, to draw a 50% sample from the Wintergreen1.sav data file, write and run the following code:

```
1) *
2) * This code illustrates the use of the sample
3) * command
4) *.
5) get file = 'Wintergreen1.sav.'
6) list cases.
7) sample .5.
8) list cases.
```

Lines 1–4 provide comments for this code. Line 5 reads the first Wintergreen data file, and line 6 lists the cases in that file. Line 7 of the code takes a 50% sample of the cases, and line 8 lists the sampled cases. Notice that in this example, the variable "resp_num" tells you which of the cases have been sampled.

To draw exactly 5 cases from the 10 cases in the Wintergreen1.sav data file, write and run the following code:

```
1) get file = 'Wintergreen1.sav.'
2) sample 5 from 10.
```

Note that once you draw the sample, the cases that were not sampled are no longer in the working data file.

Split File

The `split file` command is used to divide the working data file into subgroups that are then analyzed separately. The working data file must be sorted by the variable used to define the subgroup. The results for the subgroups can be either displayed in the same table or in separate tables. For example, to obtain different frequency distributions for males and females for the "advisor evaluation" variable in the Wintergreen1.sav data file, write and run the following code:

```
 1) *
 2) * This code illustrates the use of the split file
 3) * command
 4) *.
 5) get file = 'Wintergreen1.sav.'
 6) sort cases by g.
 7) split file separate by g.
 8) frequencies var = ae.
 9) split file layered by g.
10) frequencies var = ae.
11) split file off.
12) frequencies var = ae.
```

Lines 1–4 provide comments for this code. Line 5 gets the data file. Line 6 sorts the data file by gender. Line 7 splits the file and instructs SPSS to produce results in separate tables. Line 8 creates the frequency distributions. Line 9 splits the file and tells SPSS to produce results in the same table. Line 10 creates the frequency distributions. Line 11 turns the split file command off. Line 12 creates one frequency distribution that includes both males and females because the split file command is no longer in effect.

Update

The update command is used to update information in one file with information from another file or files. Cases in the first file (known as the "master" file) are updated with information from the second file (known as the "transaction" file) and additional files if there are any. Both files must be sorted in ascending order and saved as SPSS data files. The master and transaction files are then matched on a common variable. The update command is useful when some, but not all, of the data for a data set have been collected and entered and the remaining data are collected and entered at a later time. The update command is also useful when old data are being updated by new data. The update command differs from the match files command, which adds variables to an SPSS data set. It also differs from the add files command, which adds cases to an SPSS data set.

To see how the update command works, enter the third set of 10 records from the Wintergreen data set (records 21 through 30) but let the "advisor evaluation" variable be blank for the last five cases and give the "community type" variable a value of 9 for all cases. The resulting data set looks like this:

Respondent Number	AA	PE	SM	AE	R	G	C
21	46	10	1	0	0	1	9
22	91	20	2	2	1	0	9
23	85	17	2	1	1	1	9
24	48	11	1	1	2	0	9
25	81	17	1	1	1	1	9
26	74	16	2	2	1	9	
27	68	12	2	1	1	9	
28	63	12	1	0	0	9	
29	72	14	0	0	0	9	
30	99	19	1	1	0	9	

Save the data set as 'Wintergreen 3a.sav.' Next, create another data set that has three variables: "respondent number," "advisor evaluation," and "community type." Let the variable "advisor evaluation" contain missing data for the first five cases and the data for the second five cases and let the variable "community type" have the data for all the cases. The resulting data set looks like this:

Respondent Number	AE	C
21	0	0
22	0	1
23	1	1
24	0	0
25	1	0
26	1	
27	1	
28	0	
29	2	
30	1	

Save this data set as 'Wintergreen3b.sav.' Now write and run the following code (the execute command is required because update does not run unless either a procedure is run or the execute command is given):

```
 1) *
 2) * This code illustrates the use of the update
 3) * command
 4) *.
 5) get file = 'Wintergreen3a.sav.'
 6) sort cases by resp_num.
 7) save outfile = 'Wintergreen3a.sav.'
 8) get file = 'Wintergreen3b.sav.'
 9) sort cases by resp_num.
10) save outfile = 'Wintergreen3b.sav.'
11) update file = 'Wintergreen3a.sav'/
12)    file = 'Wintergreen3b.sav'/
13)    by resp_num.
14) execute.
```

Lines 1–4 provide comments for this code. Line 5 reads the data file 'Wintergreen3a.sav,' line 6 sorts the cases by the variable "resp_num," and line 7 saves the sorted file. Lines 8–10 perform similar operations for the data file 'Wintergreen3b.sav.' Line 11 starts the update command and specifies the master file, line 12 specifies the transaction file, and line 13 specifies the variable used to match the two files. Line 14 causes the syntax to be run.

Examine the resulting working data file and note that it contains values for all cases for the variable "advisor evaluation" as well as the updated values for the variable "community type." The working data file is also a new data file that is made up of information from both the master and transaction files (in this example, 'Wintergreen3a.sav' is the master file because it is the first file named on the update command). Go ahead and save this new file as 'Wintergreen3.sav.'

READING COMPLEX DATA FILES

Your data may come to you in a complex form rather than the simple form of a rectangular file in which all the records are of the same type and all the variables are in the same column for each of the cases. In this section, we examine how to handle two different types of complex data files: nested data files and grouped data files.

Nested Data Files

Let's suppose that the Wintergreen data were collected from 10 students in each of five different classes, all the records from a given class followed a different kind of record that indicated from which class those records came, and the data were entered and saved as a text file. This kind of situation commonly occurs when the data are entered using scannable forms. The data from the first 20 records would look like this (the remaining three sets of 10 records would have a similar structure):

```
C01
S01 93 19 1 2 0 0 1
S02 46 12 0 0 0 0 0
S03 57 15 1 1 0 0 0
S04 94 18 2 2 1 1 1
S05 82 13 2 1 1 1 1
S06 59 12 0 0 2 0 0
S07 61 12 1 2 0 0 0
S08 29 09 0 0 1 1 0
S09 36 13 1 1 0 0 0
S10 91 16 2 2 1 1 0
C02
S11 55 10 0 0 1 0 0
S12 58 11 0 1 0 0 0
S13 67 14 1 1 0 1 1
S14 77 14 1 2 2 1 0
S15 71 12 0 0 2 1 0
S16 83 16 2 2 1 0 1
S17 96 15 2 2 2 0 1
S18 87 12 1 1 0 0 1
S19 62 11 0 0 0 0 0
S20 52 09 0 1 2 1 0
```

Notice that the first column contains a variable with different values depending on whether the record indicates class information or student information. In this example, the value of this variable is C if the record contains class information and S if the record contains student information. In the class record, the second and third columns indicate the class number. In the student records, the second and third columns indicate the respondent number. Thus, the student records are "nested" within the class records.

Go ahead and save the data from these two classes in a text file named 'WintergreenN.txt' (one way to do this would be to type the data into a word processor and then save them as a text file). Then write and run the following SPSS code to read these data:

```
 1) *
 2) * This code illustrates how to read nested data
 3) *.
 4) file type nested file = 'WintergreenN.txt'
 5)    rec = #type 1 (a).
 6) record type 'C.'
 7) data list /
 8)    class 2-3.
 9) record type 'S.'
10) data list /
11)    resp_num 2-3 aa 5-6 pe 8-9 sm 11 ae 13 r 15
12)    g 17 c 19.
13) end file type.
14) list.
```

Now let's examine each line of this code. Lines 1–3 provide comments for this code. Lines 4 and 5 use the file type command to define the type of file that will be read. Because we are reading nested data, the keyword nested has been specified. These lines also name the file to be read and define a string variable named "#type," the value of which indicates whether the record is a class record or a student record. This variable is defined as a "scratch" variable by beginning its name with the "#" character (scratch variables are not saved in the working data file). Line 6 tells SPSS that the next line will define the class records, and lines 7 and 8 use the data list command to specify the record definitions (i.e., the class number appears in columns 2 and 3). Lines 9–12 perform a similar function for the student records. Line 13 tells

SPSS that you are finished defining the file. Line 14 lists the cases that have been read.

Go ahead and run this code and examine the resulting data set. In particular, note that the value for the class record has been added to each student record so that the variable for "class" has a value of 1 for the first 10 records and a value of 2 for the second 10 records. Also note that the scratch variable "#type" does not appear in the working data file.

Grouped Data Files

Let's suppose the Wintergreen data were entered in a text file that was structured so that each case had three records. Each record begins with the "respondent number" in the first two columns and a variable that identifies the "record type" in the fourth column. In our example, the first record contains the "academic ability" and "parent education" variables, the second record contains the "student motivation" and "advisor evaluation" variables, and the third record contains the "religious affiliation," "gender," and "community type" variables. Thus, the records for each student are "grouped" together. The data from the first 10 records would look like as follows (the remaining sets of records would have a similar structure):

```
01 1 93 19
01 2 1 2
01 3 0 0 1
02 1 46 12
02 2 0 0
02 3 0 0 0
03 1 57 15
03 2 1 1
03 3 0 0 0
04 1 94 18
04 2 2 2
04 3 1 1 1
05 1 82 13
05 2 2 1
05 3 1 1 1
06 1 59 12
06 2 0 0
```

```
06 3 2 0 0
07 1 61 12
07 2 1 2
07 3 0 0 0
08 1 29 09
08 2 0 0
08 3 1 1 0
09 1 36 13
09 2 1 1
09 3 0 0 0
10 1 91 16
10 2 2 2
10 3 1 1 0
```

Go ahead and save the data from these two classes in a text file named 'WintergreenG.txt.' Then write and run the following SPSS code to read these data:

```
 1) *
 2) * This code illustrates how to read grouped data
 3) *.
 4) file type grouped
 5) file = 'c:\wintergreeng.txt'
 6)    rec = #rec 4 case = student 1-2.
 7) record type 1.
 8) data list/
 9)    aa 6-7 pe 9-10.
10) record type 2.
11) data list/
12)    sm 6 ae 8.
13) record type 3.
14) data list/
15)    r 6 g 8 c 10.
16) end file type.
17) list.
```

Now let's examine each line of this code. Lines 1 –3 provide comments for this code. Lines 4–7 use the file type command to define the type of file that will be read, which is then specified using the keyword grouped. These lines also name the file to be read and define a string variable named "#rec," the value of which indicates whether the record is the first, second, or third in the group ("#rec" is defined as a scratch variable that does not get saved in the working data file because it begins with the "#" character). Last, these lines define a variable named "student," the value of which is the respondent number ("student" is not a scratch variable and is therefore saved in the working data set because its name does not begin with the "#" character). Line 7 tells SPSS that the next line will define the first records, and lines 8 and 9 use the data list command to specify the record definitions (i.e., "academic ability" appears in columns 6 and 7 and "parent education" appears in columns 9 and 10). Lines 10–12 perform a similar function for the second records, and lines 13–15 perform a similar function for the third records. Line 16 tells SPSS that you are finished defining the file. Line 17 lists the cases that have been read.

Go ahead and run this code and examine the resulting data set. In particular, note that for each case, the three records have been combined into a single record for that case. Also note that the scratch variable "#rec" does not appear in the working data file but that the variable "student" does appear in the file.

CLEARING DATA FILES

Two commands are useful for clearing data files. The first command is new file, which is specified in syntax on a line by itself. This command clears the working data file. You can also clear the working data file using the pull-down menus in the Data Editor window (**File, New, Data**).

```
1)  *
2)  * This code illustrates how to clear the working
3)  * data file
4)  *.
5)  new file.
```

The second command is erase, which is followed by a file specification. This command deletes the specified file from the disk. For example, if you wanted to delete a file named 'tempdata.sav,' you could do so with the following syntax:

```
1) *
2) * This code illustrates how to clear the working
3) * data file
4) *.
5) erase file = tempdata.sav.
```

Use the erase command with caution because once it is executed, the specified file is gone!

DATA ENTRY FOR THE FULL WINTERGREEN DATA SET

At this point, you will want to complete data entry for the full Wintergreen data set because you will be using it in the chapters that follow. Enter all 50 cases and save them as a file called 'Wintergreen.sav.'

EXERCISE ONE

Iverson and Norpoth (1987) presented an example in which 12 subjects were randomly assigned to one of four groups. Each subject then watched a newscast about economic issues. Two of the groups watched a newscast about unemployment and two of the groups watched a newscast about inflation. Of the two groups that watched the story about unemployment, one saw a newscast with positive coverage and one saw a newscast with negative coverage. There was a similar division of the two groups that saw a newscast about inflation. After watching the newscast, subjects were asked to rate the importance of the economy as an issue on a scale of 1 to 10. The data were coded so that the type of story was coded 1 if it was about unemployment and 2 if it was about inflation, and the tone of the story was coded 1 if it was positive and 2 if it was negative.

Subject Number	Type of Story	Tone of Story	Score
01	1	1	1
02	1	1	2
03	1	1	3
04	2	1	5
05	2	1	6
06	2	1	7
07	1	2	7
08	1	2	8
09	1	2	9
10	2	2	7
11	2	2	7
12	2	2	10

Suppose that the data are entered in a nested format. The records that begin with "G" indicate the group to which the subject belongs (the first number following the "G" indicates the type of story and the second number indicates the tone of the story). The records that begin with "S" contain the subject number (two digits) and the subject's score (two digits). First, enter the data into a text file and save it as 'Norpoth87a.txt.'

G11

S0101

S0202

S0303

G21

S0405

S0506

S0607

G12

S0707

S0808

S0909

G22

S1007

S1107

S1210

Then write an SPSS program that performs the following tasks (save the program and Norpoth87.sps):

○ Reads the data.

○ Attaches a document that states "Example from Iverson and Norpoth (1987) in which subjects in four groups watched a newscast about economic issues and then rated the importance of the economy as an issue."

○ Assigns variable and value labels.

○ Displays the document.

○ Lists the cases.

○ Conducts a two-factor ANOVA to determine whether subjects'
rating of the importance of the economy as an issue depends
on whether they watched a newscast on employment or
inflation, on whether they watched a newscast with positive
or negative coverage, or on an interaction between these
two variables.

EXERCISE TWO

Now suppose instead that the data in Exercise 1 were entered in
grouped format. The first line contains the subject number, type of
story, and the tone of the story. The second line contains the
subject number and the subject's rating. Also, the type and tone of
story have been coded with an A instead of 1 and a B instead of 2.
First, enter the data into a text file and save it as 'Norpoth87b.txt.'

    011AA

    01201

    021AA

    02202

    031AA

    03203

    041BA

    04205

    051BA

    05206

    061BA

    06207

    071AB

07207

081AB

08208

091AB

09209

101BB

10207

111BB

11207

121BB

12210

Then write an SPSS program that performs the following tasks:

❍ Reads the data.

❍ Attaches a document that states "Example from Iverson and Norpoth (1987) in which subjects in four groups watched a newscast about economic issues and then rated the importance of the economy as an issue."

❍ Assigns variable and value labels.

❍ Displays the document.

❍ Uses `autorecode` to convert the type and tone of story from A and B to 1 and 2.

❍ Lists the cases.

❍ Conducts a two-factor ANOVA to determine whether subjects' rating of the importance of the economy as an issue depends on whether they watched a newscast on employment or inflation, on whether they watched a newscast with positive or negative coverage, or on an interaction between these two variables.

○ Saves the file.

○ Clears the working data set.

○ Displays the file information.

CHAPTER 3

Looping Functions

Chapter Purpose

This chapter introduces SPSS syntax that can be used to repeatedly perform a set of commands.

Chapter Goal

To introduce readers to SPSS's capabilities for writing syntax using a looped structure.

Expectation of Readers

Readers will be able to make the most use of this chapter if they are comfortable writing and running SPSS syntax, are comfortable studying SPSS syntax to discern its meaning, and are facile at relating SPSS output to the syntax that produced it. Readers are expected to write and run the SPSS code that is presented in the chapter so that they see the results of the operations.

INTRODUCTION

Looping functions can be used to repeatedly perform a set of commands. When a command only needs to be performed a small number of times, then it may be easier to simply write it in the syntax code as many times as necessary. However, if the command needs to be performed a large number of times, a looped structure is a far more efficient coding scheme (potentially saving tens or hundreds of lines of code). In addition, errors may be avoided by limiting the amount of code that needs to be written. This chapter will introduce you to the essentials of looping functions.

DO IF—END IF

The Do if—End if structure is used when you want to perform data transformations on some cases but not others. For example, suppose that the first 20 cases in the Wintergreen data set have been entered but that the coding scheme for community type changed after the data for the first 10 respondents were entered so that for the first 10 respondents, those who came from an urban area were coded 0 and those who came from a rural area were coded 1 and that the reverse was true for the second 10 respondents. To eliminate any problems in the data analyses, the second group would need to be recoded to match the scheme for the first group. The following syntax illustrates how to accomplish this purpose:

```
 1) *
 2) * This code illustrates basic "do if-end if" structure
 3) *.
 4) data list fixed/resp_num 1-2 aa 4-5 pe 6-7 sm 9 ae 10 r 11
 5) g 12 c 13.
 6) begin data.
 7) 01 9319 12001
 8) 02 4612 00000
 9) 03 5715 11000
10) 04 9418 22111
11) 05 8213 21111
12) 06 5912 00200
13) 07 6112 12000
14) 08 2909 00110
15) 09 3613 11000
16) 10 9116 22111
17) 11 5510 00101
18) 12 5811 01001
```

```
19) 13 6714 11010
20) 14 7714 12211
21) 15 7112 00211
22) 16 8316 22100
23) 17 9615 22200
24) 18 8712 11000
25) 19 6211 00001
26) 20 5209 01211
27) end data.
28) * The "do if-end if" loop follows.
29) do if (resp_num gt 10).
30) recode c (0 = 1) (1 = 0).
31) end if.
32) * The next line lists the cases.
33) list cases.
```

For convenience, this example uses data that are included within the syntax code itself. This is a feasible approach to data entry when there are a minimal number of cases and variables to be entered. Lines 1–3 provide comments for the code. Lines 4 and 5 of the code use the data list command to define the data file that will follow, the keyword fixed to inform SPSS that each variable will appear in the same column for every case, and finally specifies the columns in which each variable appears. Line 6 tells SPSS that the data follow that line, lines 7–26 contain the data itself, and line 27 tells SPSS that the last line of data has just appeared.

Chapter Glossary

Do if—End if: SPSS commands that begin and end a looped structure within which data transformations are performed on some cases but not on others.

Do repeat—End repeat: SPSS commands that begin and end a looped structure within which the same data transformations are performed on a specified set of variables.

Input program—End input program: SPSS commands that allow the user many different options for reading and transforming raw data as cases are constructed.

Loop—End loop: SPSS commands that begin and end a looped structure within which the same data transformations are performed on single cases.

```
RESP_NUM   AA      PE      SM      AE      R       G       C

   1       93      19      1       2       0       0       1
   2       46      12      0       0       0       0       0
   3       57      15      1       1       0       0       0
   4       94      18      2       2       1       1       1
   5       82      13      2       1       1       1       1
   6       59      12      0       0       2       0       0
   7       61      12      1       2       0       0       0
   8       29       9      0       0       1       1       0
   9       36      13      1       1       0       0       0
  10       91      16      2       2       1       1       1
  11       55      10      0       0       1       0       0
  12       58      11      0       1       0       0       0
  13       67      14      1       1       0       1       1
  14       77      14      1       2       2       1       0
  15       71      12      0       0       2       1       0
  16       83      16      2       2       1       0       1
  17       96      15      2       2       2       0       1
  18       87      12      1       1       0       0       1
  19       62      11      0       0       0       0       0
  20       52       9      0       1       2       1       0

 Number  of  cases  read:  20  Number  of  cases
listed:  20
```

Figure 3.1   List Cases Output From "Do if—End if" Example

Line 28 is a comment, and lines 29 to 31 contain the "do loop." Beginning with the first case, each case is tested to see if the value for "Resp_num" is greater than 10. If "Resp_num" is 10 or less, then SPSS moves on to the next case. However, if "Resp_num" is greater than 10, then the commands within the loop are executed. In our example, SPSS recodes the values for the variable "c" (community type). Once SPSS has gone through all the cases, the loop must close—this is accomplished by the third line of the looping code (i.e., line 31). Note that every line that begins with Do if must have a corresponding End if to close the loop.

Line 32 of the code is a comment, and line 33 lists the cases. Enter and run this code, then compare the output to the original data to see that the variable for community type has indeed been recoded. The output from the `list cases` command appears as shown in Figure 3.1.

An alternative method of recoding the variable for community type would be to assign new values for all cases. For example, both groups could be recoded to a common scheme, such as 3 for urban and 4 for rural. This would be accomplished by replacing the do-loop syntax in the example above with the following syntax:

```
1)  do if (resp_num le 10).
2)  recode c (0 = 3) (1 = 4).
3)  else if (resp_num gt 10).
4)  recode c (0 = 4) (1 = 3).
5)  end if.
```

Line 1 of this code starts the do loop. Beginning with the first case, each case is tested to see if the value for "Resp_num" is less than or equal to 10. If "Resp_num" is 10 or less, then line 2 recodes community type so the value of 0 becomes 3 and the value of 1 becomes 4. However, if "Resp_num" is greater than 10, SPSS skips the second line of code and moves on to line 3, where the value of "Resp_num" is again tested, but this time to see whether it is greater than 10. If so, then line 4 recodes community type so the value of 0 becomes 4 and the value of 1 becomes 3. Once SPSS has gone through all the cases, the loop must close, which is accomplished by line 5. Notice that in this example, SPSS has tested the value of "Resp_num" for every case and then executed a different data transformation depending on the result. Also, note that `else` can be used rather than `else  if` if every case that did not meet the previous test(s) is handled in the same way, as in the current example.

Do loops can also be "nested." For example, suppose Wintergreen required that students who scored below a certain point on their academic ability measure to participate in a study skills course but that the score that determined whether the student had to take the course depended on their advisor evaluation. Thus, students who were rated as 0 (fail) on their advisor evaluation have to take the course if their academic ability score is less than 80, students who were rated as 1 (succeed or fail) on their advisor evaluation have to take the course if their academic ability score is less than 60, and students who were rated as 2 (succeed) on their advisor evaluation were exempt from the course. We would like to create a new variable in the data set that indicates whether the student is required to take the study skills course. The new variable is named "course" and takes the value of 1 if the course is required and the value of 2 if it is not. The following syntax would accomplish this purpose:

```
 1) *
 2) * This code illustrates nested "do if-end if"
 3) * structure
 4) *.
 5) get file = 'c:\wintergreen.sav.'
 6) do if (ae eq 0).
 7) + do if (aa lt 80).
 8) + compute course = 1.
 9) + else if (aa ge 80).
10) + compute course = 2.
11) + end if.
12) else if (ae eq 1).
13) + do if (aa lt 60).
14) + compute course = 1.
15) + else if (aa ge 60).
16) + compute course = 2.
17) + end if.
18) else if (ae eq 2).
19) compute course = 2.
20) end if.
21) list cases = 10.
```

Lines 1–4 provide comments for this code. Line 5 starts the do loop. Beginning with the first case, each case is tested to see if the value for advisor evaluation is 0. If so, SPSS moves to line 6 and starts a second do loop, nested within the first loop. Note that the second do loop starts before SPSS encounters the end if command associated with the first do loop. Also note that the plus sign (+) is used at the beginning of the line to allow an SPSS command to be written beginning in some column other than the first one so that you can more easily read your code. Line 7 tests the case to see if the academic ability score is less than 80. If so, line 8 assigns the variable "course" a value of 1. If not, SPSS moves to lines 9 and 10 and assigns a value of 2 to the variable "course." In line 11, SPSS then reads the first end if command, which closes the nested do loop.

Next, in line 12, SPSS encounters an else if command and tests the variable for advisor evaluation to see whether it has a value of 1. As you can see, this else if command is part of the first do loop rather than the nested do loop. It is the command to which SPSS will skip (rather than going through the nested loop) if the case does not have a value of 0 for the advisor evaluation. Now if the case has a value of 1 for the advisor evaluation, then SPSS will begin the next do loop, which is again nested inside the first one. This nested loop begins with line 13 and tests the case to see if the academic ability score is less than 60, and if so, line 14 assigns the variable "course" a value of 1. If not, line 15 tests the case to see if the academic ability score is greater than 60, and if so, line 16 assigns the variable "course" a value of 2. In line 17, SPSS encounters the end if command associated with this nested do loop.

If the advisor evaluation variable does not have a value of 0 or 1, then SPSS skips both the first and second nested do loops and encounters line 18 of the code, which tests the case to see if the variable for advisor evaluation has a value of 2. If so, line 19 assigns the variable "course" a value of 2. SPSS then encounters line 20, which is the end if command that closes the original do loop. Line 21 lists the first 10 cases and produces the output shown in Figure 3.2.

Note that there are three places in this code where you could simply use the else command instead of the else if command. These are lines 9, 15, and 18, where the last alternative in each case is being tested. However, by using else if to test for a specific value, you avoid potential problems (e.g., a value of 2 being assigned to the variable "course" when in fact the variable for advisor evaluation has missing data). Note also that if you ever want to specify a condition in which SPSS is to exit the loop without going through all its commands, you can do so with the break command inside the loop.

INPUT PROGRAM—END INPUT PROGRAM

When creating a working data set, SPSS builds an input program that constructs the cases that will be included in the data set. This is done internally with commands that read data (e.g., data list and get)

```
The variables are listed in the following order:
   LINE 1:    RESP_NUM AA PE SM AE R G
   LINE 2:    C AA_REC COURSE
RESP_NUM:      1.00 93.00 19.00 1.00 2.00   .00   .00
      C:       1.00  7.00  2.00
RESP_NUM:      2.00 46.00 12.00   .00   .00   .00   .00
      C:        .00 54.00  1.00
RESP_NUM:      3.00 57.00 15.00 1.00 1.00   .00   .00
      C:        .00 43.00  1.00
RESP_NUM:      4.00 94.00 18.00 2.00 2.00 1.00 1.00
      C:       1.00  6.00  2.00
RESP_NUM:      5.00 82.00 13.00 2.00 1.00 1.00 1.00
      C:       1.00 18.00  2.00
RESP_NUM:      6.00 59.00 12.00   .00   .00 2.00   .00
      C:        .00 41.00  1.00
RESP_NUM:      7.00 61.00 12.00 1.00 2.00   .00   .00
      C:        .00 39.00  2.00
RESP_NUM:      8.00 29.00  9.00   .00   .00 1.00 1.00
      C:        .00 71.00  1.00
RESP_NUM:      9.00 36.00 13.00 1.00 1.00   .00   .00
      C:        .00 64.00  1.00
RESP_NUM:     10.00 91.00 16.00 2.00 2.00 1.00 1.00
      C:        .00  9.00  2.00
   Number of cases read: 10 Number of cases
listed: 10
```

Figure 3.2 List Cases Output From Nested Do Loop

or combine SPSS data files (e.g., add files and match files).
With the input program–end input program commands, you
can create your own input program with many options for reading and
transforming raw data. Let's see how these commands work and at the
same time examine some other new commands.

To see how the `input program–end input program` commands
function, let's imagine that the Wintergreen data were stored as a text
file and that the structure for recording the data changed at some point
in time. The "old" structure is the one with which we are already familiar, but the "new" structure records the variables after the respondent
number in reverse order (i.e., "community type" comes first and "academic
ability" comes last). The first variable in the file is called "form" and
denotes whether the case follows the old or the new structure. The data
set would look like this:

```
old01931912001

old02461200000

old03571511000

old04941822111

old05821321111

new06002001259

new07000211261

new08011000929

new09000111336

new10011221691
```

Go ahead and enter these data and save them as a text file named
"file1.dat." (Of course, you can give whatever names you wish to the
data and syntax code in this section and save them in the directory of
your choice; just be sure that the filenames in the syntax direct the program to the correct directories and files.)

Now type the following code in the SPSS syntax window and save it
as "file2.sps":

```
1) do if form = 'old.'
2) reread.
3) data list/
4)    form 1-3 (a) resp_num 4-5 aa 6-7 pe 8-9 sm 10
```

```
 5) ae 11 r 12 13 c 14.
 6) end case.
 7) else if form = 'new.'
 8) reread.
 9) data list/
10)    form 1-3 (a) resp_num 4-5 c 6 g 7 r 8 ae 9 sm
11)    10 pe 11-12 a 13-14.
12) end case.
13) end if.
```

Finally, clear the SPSS syntax window, type the following input program, and save the program as "input.sps":

```
1) input program.
2) data list file = 'file1.dat' notable/
3)    form 1-3 (a).
4) include 'file2.sps.'
5) end input program.
6) save outfile = 'file3.sav.'
```

Let's walk through the program "input.sps" to see how it works. Line 1 of the code starts the input program that encloses the data definition and transformation commands. Line 2 reads the first variable, called "form," from the raw data file (the `notable` subcommand tells SPSS not to display a table summarizing the variable definitions). Remember, this is the variable that tells us whether the case follows the old or the new structure. Line 3 begins with the `include` command. This command includes a file of SPSS commands into the syntax file currently in use. In the present example, the commands in "file2.sps" are included as if they were written as part of the "input.sps" program. The `include` command is particularly useful when you are writing multiple programs that include common sets of lengthy code. The common code can be written as a separate file and then included in the program, thereby shortening the program considerably.

At this point, SPSS acts on the code in "file2.sps." Line 1 begins a do loop that tests the variable "form" to see if it has the value "old." If so, SPSS moves to line 2 and encounters the `reread` command. This command instructs SPSS to reread a record in the data rather than moving to the next record. Lines 3 through 5 use the `data list` command to read the record using the "old" file structure. Line 6 contains the `end case` command to tell SPSS that the case is complete (a similar command not used in this example is end file, which tells SPSS that the file is complete and to stop reading data before the actual end of the file is encountered).

If line 1 of the do loop had not encountered the value "old" for the variable "form," then SPSS would have skipped to line 7 of the syntax code, the else if command, which tests the variable "form" to see if it has the value "new." If so, SPSS moves to lines 8–12 to reread the record and complete a case using the new data structure. Finally, in line 13, SPSS comes to the end if command necessary to close the do loop and returns to the "input.sps" syntax file and picks up with line 5, which contains the end input program command. This command ends the data definition and transformation commands. Finally, in line 6, SPSS encounters the save command, which causes the working data file to be saved as "file3.sav." Note that the input program–end input program commands are not executed until SPSS encounters a procedure command (such as save). If you wanted to run the program without performing a procedure, you could do so with the execute command (e.g., by substituting execute for the save command in the present example).

Go ahead and run the program now to see it function. You will end up with "file3.sav" as the active data set and it will have also been saved to your computer.

DO REPEAT—END REPEAT

The do repeat–end repeat structure repeats the same transformations on a specified set of variables. Suppose that for our Wintergreen data set we wish to create five new variables representing grades (on a scale of 1 to 4) in five different courses. At first, we do not have any data about the student grades, so we set them all to a value of 0 (because this value is outside the grading scale, we know it represents missing data and we can declare it as such). Enter and run the following syntax to see how this structure functions:

```
1) *
2) * This code illustrates "do repeat-end repeat" structure
3) *.
4) get file = 'c:\wintergreen.sav.'
```

```
5)  do repeat c = course1 to course5.
6)  compute c eq 0.
7)  end repeat.
8)  execute.
```

Lines 1–3 provide comments for this code. Line 4 reads the Wintergreen.sav data file. Line 5 starts the do-repeat loop, defines a "stand-in" variable ("c" in our example), which represents a "replacement list" of variables ("course1," "course2," "course3," "course4," and "course5" in our example). Line 6 performs the data transformation for each replacement variable represented by the stand-in variable; that is, "course1" is given the value 0, "course2" is given the value 0, and so on through "course5." Line 7 ends the loop and line 8 executes the syntax (because the do repeat–end repeat structure does not run until SPSS encounters a procedure command).

As another example, suppose the Wintergreen students are divided into three groups and we wish to create three dummy variables that contain values of 0 or 1 depending on which group the student is in (i.e., students in Group 1 have a value of 1 for the first dummy variable and a value of 0 for the second and third dummy variables). With the Wintergreen data open, create a new variable called "group" and assign some students a value of 1, some students a value of 2, and the remaining students a value of 3 for this variable. Then enter the following code in a syntax window:

```
1)  *
2)  * This code provides a second illustration of "do repeat-
3)  * end repeat" structure
4)  * Note: the Wintergreen data file must be opened and
5)  * modified as described in the text
6)  * prior to running this code
7)  *.
8)  do repeat d = dummy1 to dummy3/
9)  x = 1 to 3.
10) compute d = 0.
11) do if group = x.
12) compute d = 1.
13) end if.
14) end repeat print.
15) execute.
```

Let's examine this code to see what it does. Lines 1 through 7 provide comments for this code. Lines 8 and 9 start the do-repeat loop with stand-in variable "d" representing variables "dummy1," "dummy2," and "dummy3" and stand-in variable "x" representing values 1, 2, and 3. Line 10 sets the values of all three dummy variables to 0. Lines 11 though 13 are a do loop that executes the code inside the loop if the variable "group" has the same value as stand-in variable "x." When this is true, the dummy variable is assigned a value of 1. Line 14 ends the do-repeat loop (the print subcommand displays in the output the code executed by the loop). Line 15 executes the syntax. Run this code and look at the active data set to see that the desired variables have been created and that they have the desired values (e.g., for when "group" equals one, then "dummy1" equals 1, "dummy2" equals 0, and "dummy3" equals 0).

LOOP—END LOOP

The loop—end loop structure repeats the same transformations on single cases rather than on a set of variables (which is what the do repeat—end repeat command accomplishes). One of the simplest examples of a loop is illustrated by the following code:

```
1)  * This code illustrates "loop-end loop" structure
2)  * Note: the Wintergreen (or some other) data file must be
3)  * opened prior to running this code
4)  *.
5)  compute x = 0.
6)  loop #i = 1 to 5.
7)  compute x = x + 1.
8)  end loop.
9)  execute.
```

Lines 1–4 provide comments for this code. Line 5 of this code creates a new variable called "x" and assigns it the value of 0. Line 6 begins the loop with a scratch "indexing variable" named "i," which is incremented each time the loop is executed for a case (the "#" in front of the variable name "i" tells SPSS that this is a "scratch" variable that is not to be added to the working data file). Line 7 increments the value of the variable "x" by one with each iteration of the loop. Line 8 ends the loop, and line 9 executes the code. With the Wintergreen data file open, go ahead and enter and run this code to see that the new variable "x" has been created and that all cases have the value 5.

You can use the loop—end loop structure in much more complicated ways to read complex data files or to generate data for the working data file. Once you have the fundamental ideas presented in this chapter well in hand, I encourage you to seek more information and ideas from the *SPSS Syntax Reference Guide*. By way of example, the following code uses commands we have covered previously to generate a file with 1,000 cases, each with one variable called "newvar" that approximates a normal distribution:

```
1) *
2) * This code generates a file with 1,000 cases, each
3) * with one variable called "newvar" that
4) * approximates a normal distribution
5) *.
6) new file.
7) input program.
8) loop #i = 1 to 1000.
9) compute newvar = normal(1).
10) end case.
11) end loop.
12) end file.
13) end input program.
14) freq var = newvar/
15)    format = notable/
16)    histogram.
```

Lines 1–5 provide comments for this code. Line 6 of this code clears the working data file, and line 7 begins the input program. Line 8 begins a loop that will go through 1,000 iterations. With each iteration, the variable "newvar" will be assigned a value that is a normal pseudorandom number with a mean of zero and a standard deviation of one (this occurs in line 9 of the code). Line 10 creates a case with each iteration, line 11 completes the loop, and line 12 tells SPSS to stop building the data file once the loop is complete. Line 13 ends the input program. Lines 14–16 instruct SPSS to create a frequency distribution for

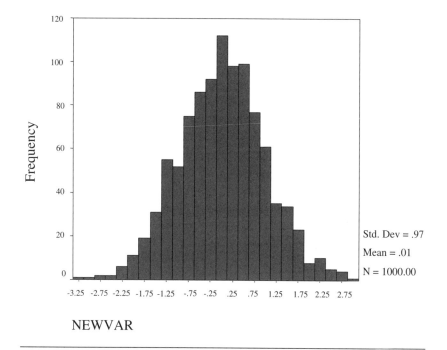

NEWVAR

Figure 3.3 Histogram of 1,000 Cases Approximating a Normal Distribution

the variable "newvar" and to display a histogram but not the frequency table. Go ahead and run this code and review the result to see how the program works. The histogram will look like the one shown in Figure 3.3.

EXERCISE THREE

Suppose that the data in Exercise 1 were entered on two different forms. The data from Form A follow the coding described in Exercise 1 (the order of the variables is subject number, form, type of story, tone of story, and score). The data from Form B are similar except that the tone of story was entered before type of story was entered. First, enter the data into a text file and save it as "Norpoth87c.txt."

01A1101

02A1102

03A1103

04A2105

05A2106

06A2107

07B2107

08B2108

09B2109

10B2207

11B2207

12B2210

Now write an SPSS program that performs the following tasks:

○ Reads the data using an `Input program`–`End input program` structure; uses code that is included from another file that invokes a do loop that reads the data using the `reread`, `end case`, `else if`, and `end if` commands; saves the data file; and lists the cases.

CHAPTER 4

Using the SPSS Macro Facility

Chapter Purpose

This chapter introduces the SPSS macro facility, which can be used to perform complex and repetitive tasks. Macros are written using SPSS syntax. However, macros use syntax in a qualitatively different manner than its basic use for reading, transforming, and analyzing data. When we work with macros, it is almost as if we are using a different language.

Chapter Goal

To provide readers with fundamental skills for writing SPSS macros.

Expectation of Readers

Readers will be able to make the most use of this chapter if they are comfortable writing and running SPSS syntax, are comfortable studying SPSS syntax to discern its meaning, and are facile at relating SPSS output to the syntax that produced it. Readers are expected to use abstract thinking skills to conceptualize how macros work. Readers are expected to write and run the SPSS code that is presented in the chapter so that they see the results of the operations.

INTRODUCTION

A macro is a set of commands that can be used to reduce the time and effort needed to perform complex and repetitive tasks. For example, macros can be used to repeatedly issue a series of commands using looping functions, specify a set of variables, produce output from several procedures using a single command, or create complex procedures. This chapter will provide you with a basic understanding of macros, a powerful command syntax feature within SPSS.

MACROS WITH NO ARGUMENTS

Let's begin with an example of a simple macro and examine it to see how it works. We will then build from there to explore macros in more detail. To begin,

○ Open the Wintergreen.sav data file and a new syntax window.

○ In the syntax window, type and run the following code:

```
1) *
2) * This code creates and calls a macro with no arguments
3) *.
4) define newfreq1 ().
5) frequencies var = sm ae r g c/
6) barchart percent.
7) !enddefine.
8) newfreq1.
```

○ View the output.

Lines 1–3 provide comments for this code. Lines 4–7 define the macro. Line 4 begins with the command define, which informs SPSS that a macro is about to be defined. The macro name follows immediately after the define command. In this example, the name of the macro is "newfreq1." The macro "arguments" are contained in the parentheses after the macro name (macro arguments are discussed below). Because there are no arguments in this macro, the parentheses are left blank; however, they are still required.

Lines 5 and 6 of the code contain the "macro body." In this example, the macro body contains syntax that tells SPSS to create frequency distributions and bar charts of percentage distributions for the five variables that are listed. Line 7 tells SPSS that the macro definition is completed. Note that all macro keywords (after define) begin with an exclamation point (!). Think of the exclamation point as indicating that you are writing macro code.

Line 8 "calls" the macro. The macro is called simply by using the name of the macro in SPSS syntax. Once called, SPSS performs a process called "macro expansion." That is, SPSS expands the macro name (in our example, "newfreq") into the strings contained in the body of the macro (in our example, "frequencies var = sm ae r g c/ barchart percent"). Once the macro has been expanded, these strings are executed as part of SPSS command syntax (i.e., the frequencies command is run for the variables "sm," "ae," "r," "g," and "c").

MACROS WITH KEYWORD ARGUMENTS

Now let's look at using a macro with arguments. We'll start with an example using a keyword argument:

○ Open the Wintergreen.sav data file and a new syntax window.

○ In the syntax window, type and run the following code.

Chapter Glossary

Argument: A variable within a macro that can accept information from outside the macro.
Define: SPSS command that begins a macro definition.
!Endefine: SPSS command that ends a macro definition.
Macro call (or simply, "**call**"): To execute a macro.
Macro expansion: The process by which SPSS expands a macro name into the strings contained in the body of the macro and then executes them as part of SPSS command syntax.
Set commands: Commands that control the SPSS environment.
Token: Information that is passed to a macro from outside the macro.

```
1) *
2) * This code creates and calls a macro with
3) * one keyword argument
4) *.
5) define newfreq2 (argvars = tokens(5)).
6) frequencies var = !argvars/
7)    barchart percent.
8) !enddefine.
9) newfreq2 argvars = sm ae r g c.
```

○ View the output.

Lines 1–4 provide comments for this code. Line 5 of this code begins the macro definition with the define command. The macro name ("newfreq2") comes immediately after the define command. This macro has one "keyword argument," which means that at the time of macro expansion, a user-defined keyword will be used to provide information to the macro. The keyword is named within the parentheses—in this example, the keyword is called "argvars," although you could give it any other name with up to seven characters that do not match an SPSS macro keyword. At the time of macro expansion, the keyword will contain five pieces of information, called "tokens," which will be passed to the macro. A token is simply something that has a particular meaning in a particular context. For example, you might give someone a card as a token of your appreciation for inviting you to dinner the previous evening. Here we are saying that within the context of this macro, the keyword "argvars" will give five tokens (i.e., pieces of information) from outside the macro to the frequencies command within the macro to let it know for which variables SPSS is to construct the frequency distributions.

Lines 6 and 7 of the code define the macro body. The macro will run the frequencies procedure using the variables that are passed to it by the keyword "argvars." Line 8 ends the macro definition. Line 9 calls the macro and specifies the tokens that are assigned to the keyword.

When this macro is called, SPSS expands the macro into the following strings:

```
frequencies var = sm ae r g c/
  barchart percent.
```

In the macro call, "argvars" is assigned the tokens "sm ae r g c," which are then passed to the macro to be included in place of "!argvars" in the expansion. Once expanded, the strings are executed as part of SPSS command syntax. SPSS computes frequency distributions and draws bar charts for the five variables listed.

Now let's look at another example of a macro with keyword arguments. This one will define two arguments, each with one token, and then use them in a crosstabs procedure. (Note that in the definition, the two arguments are separated by a slash.)

○ Open the Wintergreen.sav data file and a new syntax window.

○ In the syntax window, type and run the following code:

```
1) *
2) * This code creates and calls a macro
3) * with two keyword arguments
4) *.
5) define mycross (myrow = !tokens(1)/
6)                 mycol = !tokens(1)).
7) crosstabs tables = !myrow by !mycol/
8)    cells = count row.
9) !enddefine.
10) mycross myrow = g mycol = sm.
11) mycross myrow = c mycol = ae.
```

○ View the output.

Lines 1–4 provide comments for this code. Lines 5 and 6 start the macro definition, name the macro "mycross," name the first argument "myrow" and give it one token, and name the second argument "mycol" and give it one token. Lines 7 and 8 define the macro body. The macro will run the crosstabs procedure using the variables that are passed to it by the keywords "myrow" and "mycol." Line 9 ends the macro definition. Line 10 calls the macro for the first time and specifies the tokens that are assigned to the keyword. When line 10 calls the macro, SPSS expands the macro into the following strings:

```
crosstabs tables = g by sm/
  cells = count row.
```

In this first macro call, "myrow" is assigned the token "g" and "mycol" is assigned the token "sm," and these two tokens are passed to the macro to be included in place of "!myrow" and "!mycol" in the expansion. Once expanded, the strings are executed as part of SPSS command syntax. SPSS computes a cross-tabulation of gender by student motivation.

Similarly, when line 11 calls the macro a second time, SPSS expands the macro into the following strings:

```
crosstabs tables = c by ae/
  cells = count row.
```

In this second macro call, "myrow" is assigned the token "c" and "mycol" is assigned the token "ae." These two tokens are then passed to the macro to be included in place of "!myrow" and "!mycol" in the expansion. Once expanded, the strings are executed as part of SPSS command syntax. SPSS computes a cross-tabulation of community type by advisor evaluation.

MACROS WITH POSITIONAL ARGUMENTS

A macro may have a positional argument rather than a keyword argument. That is, the arguments passed to the macro are based on their position in the macro call rather than on being assigned to a specific argument. To see how this works,

○ Open the Wintergreen.sav data file and a new syntax window.

○ In the syntax window, type and run the following code:

```
 1) *
 2) * This code creates and calls a macro
 3) * with two positional arguments
 4) *.
 5) define newdesc1 (!positional !tokens (1)/
 6)                   !positional !tokens (1)).
 7) descriptives var = !1 !2/
 8)    statistics = mean stddev min max.
 9) !enddefine.
10) newdesc1 aa pe.
11) newdesc1 pe aa.
```

○ View the output

Lines 1–4 provide comments for this code. Lines 5 and 6 of this code begin the definition of a macro named "newdesc1," which has two positional arguments, each with one token. Lines 7 and 8 of the macro instruct SPSS to run the `descriptives` procedure with the two arguments—the first argument ("!1") accepts the first token in the macro call and the second argument ("!2") accepts the second token in the macro call. Line 9 ends the macro definition. Line 10 calls the macro and passes the variable name "aa" as the first argument and the variable name "pe" as the second argument. Line 11 calls the macro again but this time passes the variable name "pe" as the first argument and the variable name "aa" as the second argument.

There are three ways to assign positional macro arguments that do not require you to know in advance how many tokens will be passed to the macro. The first uses the keyword `!charend` (*'character'*) to assign all tokens up to the specified *character* to the argument. The second uses the keyword `!enclose` (*'character,'* *'character'*) to assign all tokens between the indicated *characters* to the argument. The third uses the keyword `!cmdend` to assign all tokens up to the next command to the argument. To see how the first of these three ways to use the keywords works,

○ Open the Wintergreen.sav data file and a new syntax window.

○ In the syntax window, type and run the following code:

```
 1) *
 2) * This code creates and calls a macro with two positional
 3) * arguments using the "!charend" keyword
 4) *.
 5) define exchar (!positional !charend ('/')/
 6)                 !positional !charend ('/')).
 7) descriptives var =!1.
 8) frequencies var = !2.
 9) !enddefine.
10) exchar aa pe / sm ae r g c /.
```

○ View the output.

Lines 1–4 provide comments for this code. Lines 5 and 6 of this code begin the definition of a macro named "exchar" (short for "example of using a character to end a list of tokens") that contains two arguments, each made up of the tokens assigned up to the assigned character that indicates the end of the tokens (i.e., "/"). Line 7 tells SPSS to run the `descriptives` procedure using the first argument, and line 8 tells SPSS to run the `frequencies` procedure using the second argument. Line 9 ends the macro definition. Line 10 calls the macro and assigns the variable names "aa" and "pe" to the first argument (because "pe" is followed by the character that defines the end of the tokens assigned to the first argument) and assigns the variable names "sm," "ae," "r," "g," and "c" to the second argument (because "c" is followed by the character that defines the end of the tokens assigned to the second argument).

Now let's take a look at the second way to use these keywords:

○ Open the Wintergreen.sav data file and a new syntax window.

○ In the syntax window, type and run the following code:

```
 1) *
 2) * This code creates and calls a macro with two positional
 3) * arguments using the "!enclose" keyword
 4) *.
 5) define exencl (!positional !enclose ('(',')')/
 6)                !positional !enclose ('(',')')).
 7) descriptives var =!1.
 8) frequencies var = !2.
 9) !enddefine.
10) exencl (aa pe) (sm ae r g c).
```

○ View the output.

Lines 1–4 provide comments for this code. Lines 5 and 6 begin the definition of a macro named "exencl" (short for "example of using a character to enclose a list of tokens") that contains two arguments, each made up of the tokens assigned by being enclosed within the defined characters—the first character is the open parenthesis "(" and the second character is the close parenthesis ")". Line 7 tells SPSS to run the `descriptives` procedure using the first argument, and line 8 tells SPSS to run the `frequencies` procedure using the second argument. Line 9 ends the macro definition. Line 10 calls the macro and assigns the variable names "aa" and "pe" to the first argument (because they are enclosed within the defined characters—the open parenthesis and the close parenthesis) and assigns the variable names "sm," "ae," "r," "g," and "c" to the second argument (again because they are enclosed within the defined characters—the open parenthesis and the close parenthesis).

Now let's take a look at the third way to use these keywords:

○ Open the Wintergreen.sav data file and a new syntax window.

○ In the syntax window, type and run the following code:

```
 1) *
 2) * This code creates and calls a macro with two positional
 3) * arguments using the "!charend" keyword
 4) *.
 5) define excmdend (!positional !charend ('/')/
 6)                   !positional !cmdend).
 7) descriptives var =!1.
 8) frequencies var = !2.
 9) !enddefine.
10) excmdend aa pe/ sm ae r g c.
```

○ View the output.

Lines 1–4 provide comments for this code. Lines 5 and 6 of this code begin the definition of a macro named "excmdend" (short for "example of assigning tokens to the end of the command") that contains two arguments, the first made up of the tokens assigned up to the assigned character that indicates the end of the tokens (i.e., "/") and the second made up of the remaining tokens up to the end of the command. Line 7 tells SPSS to run the `descriptives` procedure using the first argument, and line 8 tells SPSS to run the `frequencies` procedure using the second argument. Line 9 ends the macro definition. Line 10 calls the macro and assigns the variable names "aa" and "pe" to the first argument (because "pe" is followed by the character that defines the end of the tokens assigned to the first argument) and assigns the variable names "sm," "ae," "r," "g," and "c" to the second argument (because they are the remaining tokens up to the end of the command).

STRING MANIPULATION AND LOOPING CONSTRUCTS

A macro can use string manipulation functions to process character strings and to produce new character strings. As an example of macro string manipulation, the command !concat(string1, sting2) creates a string that is the concatenation of the two strings within the parentheses. To illustrate, !concat(v,temp) creates the string "vtemp." You may find a complete list of macro string manipulation functions in the *SPSS Syntax Reference Guide* or by using the "Help" menu.

You can also write macro loops to accomplish repetitive tasks. The macro loop begins with the command !do and ends with the command !doend. The loop repeats as many times as instructed.

To understand how these two features work, imagine that you want to create 10 new variables in the working data file, each of which contains values of a random number drawn from a normal distribution with a mean of zero and a standard deviation of one:

○ Open the Wintergreen.sav data file and a new syntax window.

○ In the syntax window, type and run the following code:

```
1) *
2) * This code creates and calls a macro that illustrates
3) * macro string manipulation and a macro do loop
4) *.
5) define randvars (arg1 = !tokens(1)/
6)                   arg2 = !tokens(1)).
7) !do !i = !arg1 !to !arg2.
8) compute !concat(r,!i,var) = normal (1).
9) !doend.
10) !enddefine.
11) randvars arg1 = 1 arg2 = 10.
12) execute.
```

○ View the Data Editor window to see the 10 new variables and their values.

Lines 1–4 provide comments for this code. Lines 5 and 6 of this code begin the definition of a macro named "randvars" (for "random variables") that has two keyword arguments (named "arg1" and "arg2"), each with one token. Line 7 begins the loop with the command !do, assigns the variable "!i" as the *index* for the loop (i.e., "!i" will be incremented by one each time the loop goes through a cycle to keep track of which cycle the loop is on), and instructs the loop to cycle as many times as indicated by "!arg1" and "!arg2." Line 8 creates new numeric variables; each variable name is made up of "r" (for "random"), the number of the cycle the loop is on, and "var" (for "variable"). Line 9 ends the loop, and line 10 ends the macro definition. Line 11 calls the macro and assigns the value 1 to the first argument and the value 10 to the second argument. Line 12 executes the pending transformations (the assignment of values to the variables).

When this macro is called, it cycles through the loop 10 times. The first time through, it creates a new numeric variable named "v1temp"; the second time through, it creates a new numeric variable named "v2temp"; and so on, until the 10th (and last) time through, when it creates a new numeric variable named "v10temp." Look at your working data file to see that the new variables have been created.

Notice that this example illustrates the power of macros to perform repetitive tasks. Rather than using the macro to create the 10 new variables, we could have written 10 lines of code, one to create each new variable:

```
compute r1var = normal(1).
compute r2var = normal(1).
  . . .
compute r3var = normal(1).
execute.
```

However, we were able to save three lines of code by writing the macro (eight lines long) rather than one line for each new variable. This example does not save much time in terms of writing SPSS syntax. But consider that by simply letting "arg2" equal 100 instead of 10, we can save 93 lines of code as well as considerable time and tedium!

COMMENTING AND MACROS

I encourage you to make liberal use of comments throughout your SPSS code. Macro comments will help you keep track of what your code does and why you wrote it to perform those functions. It will also be helpful to others who read your code.

There are a number of ways to include comments in SPSS syntax. One common way is to begin a line with an asterisk (*). All SPSS syntax following the asterisk is ignored until a period (.) is reached. However, macros are expanded when their name is written in a comment beginning with an asterisk. If you wish to use the macro name in a comment, enclose the comment between slashes and asterisks:

```
/* comment goes here, including macro name */.
```

Similarly, you can provide comments within your macro:

```
 1) *
 2) * This code illustrates commenting within a macro
 3) *.
 4) define tempvars (arg1 = !tokens(1)/
 5)                   arg2 = !tokens(1)) /* define macro */.
 6) !do !i = !arg1 !to !arg2              /* begin loop */.
 7) numeric !concat(v,!i,temp)            /* create vars */.
 8) !doend                                /* end loop */.
 9) !enddefine                            /* end define */.
10) tempvars arg1 = 1 arg2 = 10           /* call macro */.
```

SET COMMANDS FOR MACROS

There are four SET commands that you can use with macros. The first macro set command is MPRINT, which is set to either YES or NO. If this command is set to YES, then the SPSS output will display a list of commands after macro expansion. The second command is MEXPAND, which is set to either ON or OFF. If this command is set to OFF, then macros are not expanded. The third command is MNEST, which specifies the number of levels a macro can be nested (i.e., the number of macros you can write *within* a macro). The fourth command is MITERATE, which specifies the maximum number of loop iterations within macro expansion.

HELP WITH MACROS

There are three very good sources for macro help, of which I encourage you to make use. The first source is the *SPSS Syntax Reference Guide.* This guide will provide you with additional information about macros and help you build your macro skills. The second source is the help file available through the SPSS pull-down menu. The third source is the "macro library" available on the SPSS web site (http://www.spss.com/tech/stat/Macros/). The macro library will provide you with many additional examples of macros from which you will learn a great deal if you take the time to study them.

EXERCISE FOUR

With the ANOVA in Exercise 1 in mind, write a macro with keyword arguments that accepts two tokens, each representing one of the two factors, and runs the analysis.

EXERCISE FIVE

Rewrite the macro in Exercise 4 so that it has positional rather than keyword arguments.

CHAPTER 5

Working With Pivot Tables

Chapter Purpose

This chapter covers key features of SPSS pivot tables, including transposing rows and columns, working with pivot table layers, formatting and bookmarking pivot tables, and applying TableLooks.

Chapter Goal

To provide readers skills for modifying SPSS pivot tables. Additional skills for working with SPSS pivot tables will be explored in Chapter 8 on using the SPSS scripting facility.

Expectation of Readers

Readers will be able to make the most use of this chapter if they are familiar with creating and interpreting tabular output. Readers are expected to generate the pivot tables shown in the chapter and practice modifying them as described.

INTRODUCTION

So far in this book, we have covered a variety of SPSS syntax features that may be used to work with data. Ultimately, analytic procedures are applied to these data and output is produced. Many SPSS procedures produce results that appear in the Output Viewer as pivot tables. These results display information in rows, columns, and layers that can be exchanged (i.e., a row can be made a column and a column can be made a row). The Pivot Table Editor can also be used to modify pivot tables. This chapter covers key features of pivot tables.

First, let's create a pivot table with which to work.

○ Open the Wingtergreen.sav data set.

○ Write and run the following syntax to create a cross-tabulation of gender by student motivation by community type (i.e., community type is the "layer"), with cells that contain counts and row percentages (or use the pull-down menus to create the cross-tabulation, if you prefer):

```
1) *
2) * This code creates a cross-tabulation of
3) * gender by student motivation
4) *.
5) crosstabs tables = g by sm by c/ cells = count row.
```

The resulting pivot table is shown in Figure 5.1. This pivot table compares males and females in their level of student motivation, depending on whether they come from an urban or a rural community.

TRANSPOSING ROWS AND COLUMNS

Now let's see how we can work with the pivot table so that it presents the results in different ways.

○ First, double-click the pivot table to activate it.

Now, let's say we would like to view the result in column format rather than row format. To move all the rows to columns and all the columns to rows,

○ Select **Pivot, Transpose Rows and Columns** from the menu.

G Gender * SM Student Motivation * C Community Type Cross Tabulation

C Community Type				SM Student Motivation			Total
				.00 Not Willing	1.00 Undecided	2.00 Willing	
.00 Urban	G Gender .00 Male		Count	8	6	3	17
			% within G Gender	47.1%	35.3%	17.6%	100.0%
		1.00 Female	Count	3	7	3	13
			% within G Gender	23.1%	53.8%	23.1%	100.0%
	Total		Count	11	13	6	30
			% within G Gender	36.7%	43.3%	20.0%	100.0%
1.00 Rural	G Gender .00 Male		Count	1	7	3	11
			% within G Gender	9.1%	63.6%	27.3%	100.0%
		1.00 Female	Count	1	3	5	9
			% within G Gender	11.1%	33.3%	55.6%	100.0%
	Total		Count	2	10	8	20
			% within G Gender	10.0%	50.0%	40.0%	100.0%

Figure. 5.1 Gender by Student Motivation by Community Type Cross-Tabulation

The resulting table, which displays the same information but in transposed format, is shown in Figure 5.2. Now

○ Select **Pivot, Transpose Rows and Columns** again.

You will see that the table returns to its original format (as shown in Figure 5.1).

Now let's use the Pivot Tray to modify the table.

○ Double-click the pivot table to activate it.

○ Select **Pivot, Pivoting Trays** from the menu.

Chapter Glossary

Bookmark: Bookmarks save the format of a table.

Pivot table: SPSS tabular output in which rows, columns, and layers can be exchanged.

Pivot tray: SPSS graphic in which exchangeable icons represent row, column, and layer dimensions of a table.

TableLook: A collection of table properties that may be applied in their entirety to a table.

G Gender * SM Student Motivation * C Community Type Cross Tabulation

		.00 Urban						1.00 Rural					
		G Gender						G Gender					
		.00 Male		1.00 Female		Total		.00 Male		1.00 Female		Total	
		Count	% within G Gender	Count	% within G Gender	Count	% within G Gender	Count	% within G Gender	Count	% within G Gender	Count	% within G Gender
SM Student Motivation	.00 Not Willing	8	47.1%	3	23.1%	11	36.7%	1	9.1%	1	11.1%	2	10.0%
	1.00 Undecided	6	35.3%	7	53.8%	13	43.3%	7	63.6%	3	33.3%	10	50.0%
	2.00 Willing	3	17.6%	3	23.1%	6	20.0%	3	27.3%	5	55.6%	8	40.0%
Total		17	100.0%	13	100.0%	30	100.0%	11	100.0%	9	100.0%	20	100.0%

Figure 5.2 Transposed Rows and Columns for Figure 5.1.

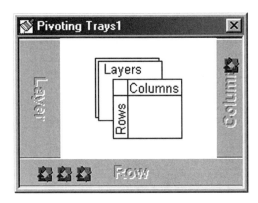

Figure 5.3 Pivoting Trays

The Pivoting Tray window opens, as shown in Figure 5.3. The pivoting trays contain icons representing the row, column, and layer dimensions of the table. Hold the mouse pointer over the icons to see what they represent.

To change the arrangement of the table,

○ Drag the icons you wish to change to the area of the tray to which you wish to change them or to change the order in which they are displayed.

For example, to compare student motivation for people within community type, depending on their gender, drag the gender icon in the row tray so that it appears before the community type icon. To obtain the table illustrated in Figure 5.2, drag both the community type and gender icons from the row tray to the column tray and drag the student motivation icon from the column tray to the row tray. This shows you that the "Transpose Rows and Columns" menu choice has the effect of moving all row icons to the column tray and all column icons to the row tray.

WORKING WITH PIVOT TABLE LAYERS

Now let's look at working with layers. Return the table so that it looks like it originally did in Figure 5.1.

G Gender * SM Student Motivation * C Community Type Crosstabulation

C Community Type: .00 Urban

			SM Student Motivation			
			.00 Not willing	1.00 Undecided	2.00 Willing	Total
G Gender	.00 Male	Count	8	6	3	17
		% within G Gender	47.1%	35.3%	17.6%	100.0%
	1.00 Female	Count	3	7	3	13
		% within G Gender	23.1%	53.8%	23.1%	100.0%
Total		Count	11	13	6	30
		% within G Gender	36.7%	43.3%	20.0%	100.0%

Figure 5.4 Layered Pivot Table

○ Select **Pivot, Reset Pivots to Defaults** from the menu.

This choice resets changes that are the result of pivoting actions but does not reset other changes that have been made to the table.

○ Now open the Pivoting Trays and drag the community type icon from the row tray to the layer tray.

The resulting pivot table is shown in Figure 5.4.

Notice that the gender variable is no longer shown within each value of the community type variable, as it was in Figure 5.1. Rather, it is as if SPSS has created two tables cross-tabulating gender by student motivation, one for each value of community type. The two tables are "layered" one upon the other, with the top layer visible. To move from one layer to another,

○ Activate the pivot table.

○ Select **Pivot, Go to Layer . . .** from the menu.

The dialog box shown in Figure 5.5 will appear.

To change from the layer for the urban community type to the rural community type, click "Rural" in the "Categories for Community type" on the right-hand side of the dialog box and then click "OK." Look at the pivot table and notice that it has changed to the layer for the rural community type. This feature is particularly helpful when you have layer variables with many values. (Note that as an alternative, you can change

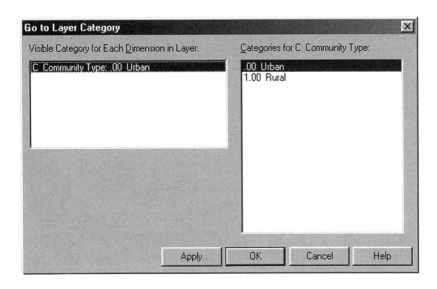

Figure 5.5 Go to Layer Category Dialog Box

layers by selecting them from the drop-down list next to the layer variable name just above the upper left corner of the table.)

FORMATTING PIVOT TABLES

There are many different ways to modify a pivot table format. Let's make several modifications to the pivot table to begin exploring the options. First, let's hide the labels for the community type, gender, and statistics dimensions.

❍ Double-click the pivot table to activate it.

❍ Click on either the "community type," "urban," or "rural" label.

❍ Select **View, Hide Dimension Label** from the menu.

Notice that the "community type" label at the upper left corner of the table is now hidden. Repeat the operation for the gender and statistics dimensions and notice that the table now looks as shown in Figure 5.6. Now let's undo these changes.

				SM Student Motivation			
				.00 Not Willing	1.00 Undecided	2.00 Willing	Total
.00 Urban	G Gender	.00 Male	Count	8	6	3	17
			% within G Gender	47.1%	35.3%	17.6%	100.0%
		1.00 Female	Count	3	7	3	13
			% within G Gender	23.1%	53.8%	23.1%	100.0%
	Total		Count	11	13	6	30
			% within G Gender	36.7%	43.3%	20.0%	100.0%
1.00 Rural	G Gender	.00 Male	Count	1	7	3	11
			% within G Gender	9.1%	63.6%	27.3%	100.0%
		1.00 Female	Count	1	3	5	9
			% within G Gender	11.1%	33.3%	55.6%	100.0%
	Total		Count	2	10	8	20
			% within G Gender	10.0%	50.0%	40.0%	100.0%

Figure 5.6 Pivot Table With Hidden Dimension Labels

○ Click where the dimension label is located or on a value for the dimension you wish to show.

○ Choose **View, Show Dimension Label** from the menu.

Alternatively, to show all of the dimension labels you can

○ Choose **View, Show All** from the menu.

Similarly, you can show and hide categories (i.e., entire rows or columns) and category labels without hiding data cells, footnotes, titles, and captions.

Now let's rotate the row and column labels in the table.

○ Double-click the table to activate it.

○ Choose **Format, Rotate Inner Row Labels** from the menu.

○ Choose **Format, Rotate Inner Row Labels** from the menu once again to return the labels to their original positions.

○ Select **Format, Rotate Outer Column Labels** from the menu to see how it changes the table.

The resulting table is shown in Figure 5.7. Note that only the inner-most rows and outermost columns can be rotated.

G Gender * SM Student Motivation * C Community Type Cross Tabulation

| | | | | SM Student Motivation | | | |
				.00 Not Willing	1.00 Undecided	2.00 Willing	Total
.00 Urban	G Gender	.00 Male	Count	8	6	3	17
			% within G Gender	47.1%	35.3%	17.6%	100.0%
		1.00 Female	Count	3	7	3	13
			% within G Gender	23.1%	53.8%	23.1%	100.0%
	Total		Count	11	13	6	30
			% within G Gender	36.7%	43.3%	20.0%	100.0%
1.00 Rural	G Gender	.00 Male	Count	1	7	3	11
			% within G Gender	9.1%	63.6%	27.3%	100.0%
		1.00 Female	Count	1	3	5	9
			% within G Gender	11.1%	33.3%	55.6%	100.0%
	Total		Count	2	10	8	20
			% within G Gender	10.0%	50.0%	40.0%	100.0%

Figure 5.7   Pivot Table With Outer Column Labels Rotated

Let's add a pivot table caption and a pivot table footnote, and then let's change the marker used to indicate the footnote.

❍ Double-click the table to activate it.

❍ Select **Insert, Caption** from the menu.

The caption will appear at the bottom of the pivot table and will simply say "Table Caption." You can select this text and then type the caption you wish.

To add a footnote to the table,

❍ Double-click the table to activate it.

❍ Click on the title, cell, or caption you wish to footnote.

❍ Select **Insert, Footnote . . .** from the menu.

The footnote appears at the bottom of the table and simply says "Footnote." You can select this text and then type the footnote you wish.

You can also use characters other than numbers or letters as your pivot table footnote markers. To use a character of your choice,

○ Double-click the table to activate it.

○ Choose **Format, Footnote Marker . . .** from the menu.

○ The Footnote Marker dialog box appears and prompts you for the marker you wish to use.

○ Choose "special marker," enter a character of your choice, and click "OK."

Notice that the footnote marker has changed both in the table and in the footnote.

You have several options for controlling the display in a cell. To alter the font of one or more cells,

○ Double-click the table to activate it.

○ Select the cells you wish to modify.

○ Choose **Format, Font . . .** from the menu.

The Font dialog box will appear. This dialog box allows you to apply the font, style, size, color, and script you wish to the selected cell(s). It also allows you to hide or underline the text in the cell. Go ahead and explore how your selections in this dialog box affect the cells.

Similarly, you have several options for controlling the cell properties of the pivot table. To alter the properties of one or more cells,

○ Double-click the table to activate it.

○ Select the cells you wish to modify.

○ Choose **Format, Cell Properties . . .** from the menu.

The Cell Properties dialog box shown in Figure 5.8 will appear. This dialog box allows you to control the display of cell values, alignment of text within the cell, the margins within the cell, and the extent to which the cell is shaded. As you did with the Cell Font dialog box, go ahead and explore how your selections in the Cell Properties dialog box affect the cells.

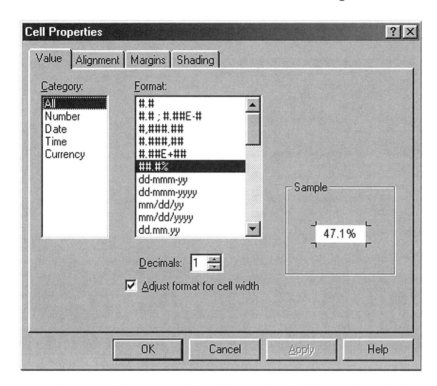

Figure 5.8   Cell Properties Dialog Box

You can also control many of the properties of the entire pivot table. To modify properties of the entire table,

○ Double-click the table to activate it.

○ Select **Format, Table Properties . . .** from the menu.

The Table Properties dialog box shown in Figure 5.9 is displayed.

This dialog box provides you with five different tabs that control many table properties. The "General" tab controls whether empty rows and columns are hidden, the placement of row dimension labels, and the width of the columns. The "Footnotes" tab lets you choose whether footnotes are alphabetic or numeric and whether they are superscripted or subscripted. The "Cell Formats" tab lets you select different areas of the table (title, layers label, corner labels, column labels, row labels,

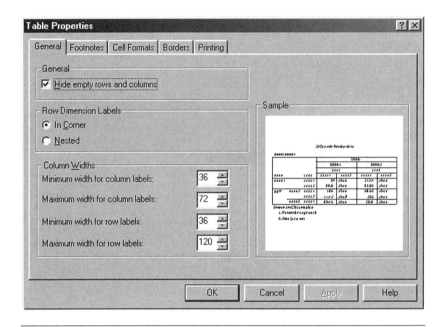

Figure 5.9 Table Properties Dialog Box

data, captions, and footnotes) and apply formatting to those areas. The "Borders" tab lets you apply different borders to the table. The "Printing" tab lets you choose whether to print all layers in a multilayer table or only the top layer. It also allows you to automatically resize a wide table or a long table to fit on a printed page. This is helpful in keeping wide (or long) tables from spilling onto multiple tables, thus making them easier to read. Now, as you did with the Cell Font and Cell Properties dialog boxes, go ahead and explore how your selections in the Table Properties dialog box affect the pivot table.

BOOKMARKING PIVOT TABLES

You can bookmark different views of your pivot table. Bookmarks save row, column, and layer dimensions, the order in which elements in each dimension are saved, and the currently displayed layer for each element. To bookmark a view of your table,

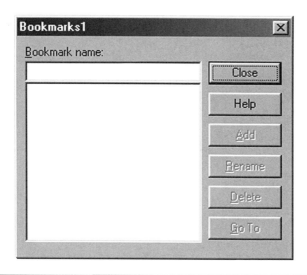

Figure 5.10   Pivot Table Bookmarks Dialog Box

○   Double-click the table to activate it.

○   Choose **Pivot, Bookmarks . . .** from the menu.

The Bookmarks dialog box shown in Figure 5.10 appears. Enter a name for your bookmark and then click "Add." Later, to show a book-marked view of a pivot table, activate the pivot table.

○   Double-click the table to activate it.

○   Choose **Pivot, Bookmarks . . .** from the menu.

○   Click the name of the bookmark you wish to select.

○   Click "Go To."

The pivot table will then take on the bookmarked view. You can also use the Bookmark dialog box to rename bookmarks: Click the name of the book-mark, click "Rename," enter the new bookmark name, and click "OK."

TABLELOOKS

So far, we have changed the appearance of a pivot table by modifying the properties of different parts of the table. You can also change the

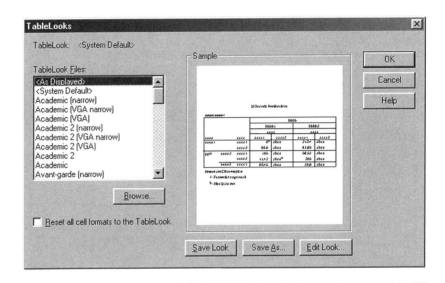

Figure 5.11 TableLooks Dialog Box

appearance of a pivot table by applying different "TableLooks." A TableLook is simply a collection of table properties. You can select one of the many TableLooks SPSS provides, or you may create and save the TableLook that meets your individual tastes and needs. To apply a TableLook,

○ Double-click the table to activate it.

○ Choose **Format, TableLooks . . .** from the menu.

The TableLooks dialog box shown in Figure 5.11 will appear.

TableLooks are saved in files and you may select any one of the TableLooks SPSS provides by clicking on its name in the "TableLooks Files." Each time you click a different filename, the "Sample" shows you how the pivot table will appear with that TableLook applied. If none of these TableLooks meets your needs, you can click "Edit Look . . . " to reveal the Table Properties dialog box, make the changes that you wish, and click "OK" once you have completed your changes to return to the TableLooks dialog box. If you click "OK" at that point, the dialog box will close and the table look will be applied to the pivot table. Note that the TableLook applies only to the activated table and that you must also apply it to other tables if you wish them to have that look.

However, if you will be using this TableLook again, it will be easier to save the TableLook than to create it each time you want to apply it. To save the TableLook, click "Save As . . . " in the TableLook dialog box. You will be prompted with the "Save As" dialog box, in which you can enter a filename and select a directory for your TableLook file. Note that TableLook files end with a ".tlo" file extension.

You may find a TableLook that you prefer for most of your pivot tables. If so, you can instruct SPSS to automatically use this TableLook when you start your SPSS session.

❍   Select **Edit, Options . . .** from the menu and you will be presented with the "SPSS Options" dialog box.

❍   Select the "Pivot Tables" tab.

❍   Click your desired TableLook filename.

❍   Click "OK."

The selected TableLook is the one that will be applied from that point forward unless you return to this tab and choose another one.

COMMAND SYNTAX FOR CONTROLLING PIVOT TABLES

You can use the set syntax command to control many aspects of the environment of your SPSS session. One of the aspects you can control is specifying which TableLook will be applied to a pivot table. Use the set command to indicate which file contains the TableLook you wish to use (if you set TLOOK None, the system default TableLook will be applied). All pivot tables that follow will have that TableLook until you use the set command to invoke a different TableLook. To see how this works,

❍   Open the Wintergreen.sav data file.

Enter and run the following syntax (make sure the path name you provide is the one that actually points to the location of your TableLook files):

```
1) *
2) * This code produces two cross-tabulations of gender
```

G Gender * SM Student motivation * C Community type Cross Tabulation

| | | | | SM Student Motivation | | | |
				.00 Not Willing	1.00 Undecided	2.00 Willing	Total
C Community type							
.00 Urban	G Gender	.00 Male	Count	8	6	3	17
			% within G Gender	47.1%	35.3%	17.6%	100.0%
		1.00 Female	Count	3	7	3	13
			% within G Gender	23.1%	53.8%	23.1%	100.0%
	Total		Count	11	13	6	30
			% within G Gender	36.7%	43.3%	20.0%	100.0%
1.00 Rural	G Gender	.00 Male	Count	1	7	3	11
			% within G Gender	9.1%	63.6%	27.3%	100.0%
		1.00 Female	Count	1	3	5	9
			% within G Gender	11.1%	33.3%	55.6%	100.0%
	Total		Count	2	10	8	20
			% within G Gender	10.0%	50.0%	40.0%	100.0%

Figure 5.12 Cross-Tabulation With Academic TableLook

```
3) * by student motivation, within community type
4) * The "academic" TableLook is applied to the first
5) * cross-tabulation
6) * The "boxed" TableLook is applied to the first
7) * cross-tabulation
8) *.
9) set tlook 'c:\program files\spss\looks\academic.tlo.'
10) crosstabs tables = g by sm by c/
11)    cells = count row.
12) set tlook 'c:\program files\spss\looks\boxed.tlo.'
13) crosstabs tables = g by sm by c/
14)    cells = count row.
```

Lines 1–8 provide comments for this code. Line 9 applies the "academic" TableLook to pivot tables. Lines 10 and 11 create a cross-tabulation of gender by student motivation by community type. Line 12 of this code applies the "boxed" TableLook to pivot tables. Lines 13 and 14 again create a cross-tabulation of gender by student motivation by community type. You will see that the pivot table produced by the first cross-tabulation procedure has the "Academic" TableLook applied to it, as illustrated in Figure 5.12.

G Gender * SM Student motivation * C Community type Cross Tabulation

C Community type					SM Student Motivation			Total
					.00 Not Willing	1.00 Undecided	2.00 Willing	
.00 Urban	G Gender	.00 Male	Count		8	6	3	17
			% within G Gender		47.1%	35.3%	17.6%	100.0%
		1.00 Female	Count		3	7	3	13
			% within G Gender		23.1%	53.8%	23.1%	100.0%
	Total		Count		11	13	6	30
			% within G Gender		36.7%	43.3%	20.0%	100.0%
1.00 Rural	G Gender	.00 Male	Count		1	7	3	11
			% within G Gender		9.1%	63.6%	27.3%	100.0%
		1.00 Female	Count		1	3	5	9
			% within G Gender		11.1%	33.3%	55.6%	100.0%
	Total		Count		2	10	8	20
			% within G Gender		10.0%	50.0%	40.0%	100.0%

Figure 5.13 Cross-Tabulation With Boxed TableLook

You will also see that the pivot table produced by the second cross-tabulation procedure has the "Boxed" TableLook applied to it, as illustrated in Figure 5.13.

You can also use the set command to control the display of variables and values in the Viewer outline and tables as follows:

○ Use "SET OVARS = labels" to display variable names in the outline, use "SET OVARS = names" to display variable names in the outline, and use "SET OVARS = both" to display variable names and labels in the outline.

○ Use "SET ONUMBERS = labels" to display value names in the outline, use "SET ONUMBERS = values" to display variable values in the outline, and use "SET ONUMBERS = both" to display value names and values in the outline.

○ Use "SET TVARS = labels" to display variable names in tables, use "SET TVARS = names" to display variable names in tables, and use "SET TVARS = both" to display variable names and labels in tables.

○ Use "SET TNUMBERS = labels" to display value names in tables, use "SET TNUMBERS = values" to display variable values in tables, and use "SET TNUMBERS= both" to display value names and values in tables.

Last, you can control the column width for pivot tables using set, as follows:

○ Use "SET TFIT = both" to adjust column width to accommodate both labels and data. Use SET "TFIT = label" to adjust column width to accommodate labels only (this produces more compact tables, but data values wider than the column are displayed as asterisks).

The following syntax illustrates the use of these set commands to control how variables and their values are displayed in the outline and tables. Enter and run this syntax and then modify and rerun it with the options described above. Compare the different output to see the effects of these set commands.

```
 1) *
 2) * This code illustrates the use of "set" commands to control
 3) * how variables and their values are displayed in the
 4) * outline and in tables.
 5) *.
 6) * display variable names in the outline.
 7) set ovars = names.
 8) * display value names in the outline.
 9) set onumbers = labels.
10) * display variable names in tables.
11) set tvars = labels.
12) * display value names in tables.
13) set tnumbers = labels.
14) * adjust column width to accommodate both labels and data
15) set tfit = both.
16) crosstabs tables = g by sm by c/
17)     cells= count row.
```

Let's examine this code to see how it works. Lines 1–8 provide comments for this code (as are the following lines that begin with an asterisk). Line 9 of this code tells SPSS to display variable names in the outline, and line 10 tells SPSS to display value names in the outline. Line 11 of this code tells SPSS to display variable names in the tables, and line 13 tells SPSS to display value names in the tables. Line 15 tells SPSS to adjust table column width to accommodate both labels and data. Lines 16 and 17 run the cross-tabulation procedure.

EXERCISE SIX

Using the data from the Wintergreen study, cross-tabulate gender by advisor evaluation and produce a pivot table showing the counts and row percentages in the cells. Obtain a chi-square statistic. Transpose the rows and columns using the pull-down menus. Transpose the rows and columns back using the pivoting trays. Rotate the inner column labels. Add a caption that states "Advisor evaluations were similar for males and females." Bookmark the pivot table view. Reset the pivot table to its original view. Return to the bookmarked view.

CHAPTER 6

Using the SPSS Interactive Graphics Feature

Chapter Purpose

This chapter introduces readers to the SPSS interactive graphics feature.

Chapter Goal

To provide readers with fundamental skills for creating and modifying SPSS interactive graphics.

Expectation of Readers

Readers will be able to make the most use of this chapter if they are familiar with creating and interpreting graphical output. Readers are expected to generate the graphics shown in the chapter and practice modifying them as described.

INTRODUCTION

Interactive charts are an SPSS feature that allows charts to be created and maintained dynamically. That is, once a chart is created, its appearance or the roles of variables in the chart can be modified, and the changes appear in the Output Viewer as soon as they are made (rather than having to wait for a procedure to be rerun). Changes can be made to the chart until it provides the illustration that best reveals the data. Interactive charts are excellent for exploring data and for use with small data files. However, some types of charts are available only as standard charts run from procedures, and for large data files, it may take more time to process interactive charts than standard ones. This chapter covers the fundamentals of SPSS interactive graphs. Once you have mastered these fundamentals, you may find a wealth of further information in the *SPSS Interactive Graphics* manual. You may also consult the *SPSS Syntax Reference Guide* if you wish to create interactive graphs from SPSS syntax (see the IGRAPH procedure).

CREATING CHARTS FROM THE GRAPH PULL-DOWN MENU

Let's begin by examining the difference in mean academic ability scores for students from the two different community types (urban and rural).

○   Open the Wintergreen data set (you need to have data in the Data Editor before you can create an interactive chart).

○   From the pull-down menu, select **Graphs, Interactive, Bar . . .**

The "Create Bar Chart" dialog box will appear (you can also create an interactive chart by selecting one from the "Insert" pull-down menu in the Output Viewer). This dialog box allows you to select the variables you wish to graph, assign labels to the graph, and select a wide variety of options for the graph. Let's begin with the "Assign Variables" tab. Notice that the source list contains the variables in the data set plus three built-in variables that allow SPSS to produce a chart of counts or percentages or a casewise chart (in which each case in the data set is represented on the axis). The type of each variable is indicated by the icon next to the variable name: Scale variables are indicated by an icon that resembles a ruler, categorical variables (both nominal and ordinal) are indicated by an icon with geometric shapes (cylinder, column, and circle), and built-in variables are indicated by an icon that resembles a cog and ruler. To select the variables for the chart, simply drag and drop them from the source list to the axis on which you want them to appear (if a variable has already been selected for that axis, dragging and dropping a variable from the source list onto the axis will cause the new and old variables to be exchanged). For example,

○ Drag the variable "aa" to the y-axis and the variable "c" to the x-axis.

○ Because community type is a categorical variable, right-click on the variable name and select "categorical" (note that the icon next to the name has changed).

○ If it is not already indicated, select "means" as the choice beneath "Bars Represent aa" (peruse the list of summary variables to see the many others that are also available).

○ Check the "Display Key" if it is not already checked.

The dialog box should now look like Figure 6.1.

Now click the "Bar Chart Options" tab. You will see options for the shape of the bars, their labels, and their baseline. For now, let's just use the options that appear by default. Next, click the "Error Bar" tab. This tab allows you to display the confidence interval of the mean, standard deviation, or standard error of the mean. It also allows you to select the shape and direction of the error bars. To enable the error bar options, click on "Display Error Bars" (but for now, let's produce a chart without them). Next, click on the "Titles" tab, which allows you to type in a chart title, chart subtitle, and caption.

Chapter Glossary

Interactive graph: SPSS graphics that are created and maintained dynamically.

ChartLook: A collection of chart properties that may be applied in their entirety to a chart.

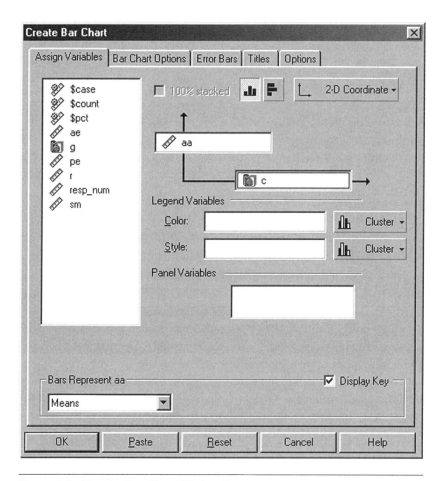

Figure 6.1 Create Bar Chart Dialog Box

○ Enter "Wintergreen Data" for the chart title.

○ Enter "Mean Academic Ability" for the chart subtitle.

○ Add "Students from rural areas displayed significantly higher mean academic ability scores than did students from urban areas" for the caption (you can confirm the significant difference by running a t test).

Finally, click the "Options" tab. This tab allows you to select the order for the categorical variable, the range for the scale variable, the look for the chart (i.e., the "ChartLook"), and the lengths of the axes. To select the scale range for the variable "aa,"

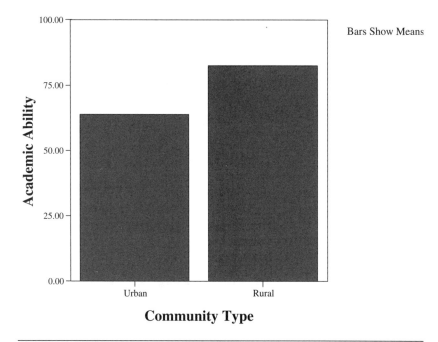

Figure 6.2 Interactive Chart of Mean Academic Ability by Community Type

○ Deselect "Auto" for the scale range for the variable "aa."

○ Enter 0 for the minimum and 100 for the maximum for the scale range for the variable "aa" (because this represents the range for this variable).

○ Otherwise, select the default options.

○ Click the OK button to obtain the chart.

Notice that the chart looks like the one in Figure 6.2 (it is possible that your chart may look a little different if you have different default options).

Now let's return to the "Create Bar Chart" dialog box. Suppose we wish to compare mean academic ability scores between males and females from within each community type.

○ Move the variable "c" to become a "Panel Variable."

○ Move the variable "g" to the x-axis (make sure that this variable is categorical by right-clicking on it and selecting this type if necessary).

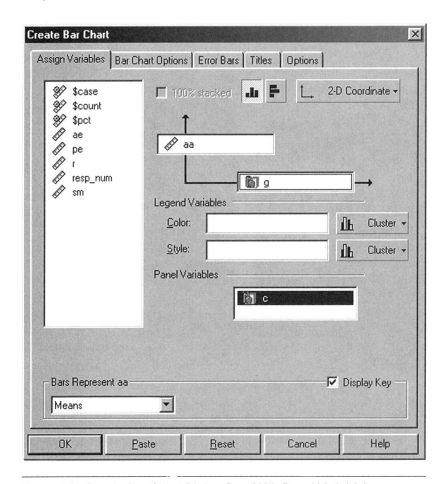

Figure 6.3 Create Bar Chart Dialog Box (With Panel Variable)

○ The dialog box now looks like Figure 6.3.

○ Click "OK" to produce the chart shown in Figure 6.4.

Notice that each community type is a panel in this chart and that mean scores for males and females are displayed within each panel. That is, males and females who come from urban communities are compared with each other, as are males and females from rural communities.

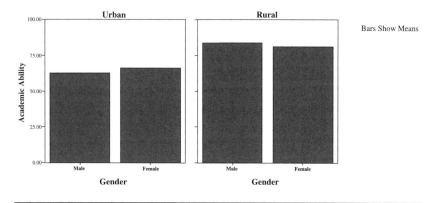

Figure 6.4 Interactive Chart of Mean Academic Ability by Gender Within Community Type

CREATING CHARTS FROM PIVOT TABLES

You can also create an interactive chart from a pivot table. Let's see how this is done by repeating the present example. To obtain the pivot table,

○ Open the Wintergreen data set.

○ From the pull-down menus, select **Analyze, Compare Means, Means . . .**

○ The "Means Dialog Box" appears; select "aa" for the dependent variable and "c" for the independent variable.

○ Click the "Options" button and select "Mean" as the only "Cell Statistic."

○ Click the "Continue" button.

○ Click the "OK" button.

You will obtain the pivot table shown in Figure 6.5.
To create an interactive graphic from the pivot table,

○ Double-click the pivot table to activate it.

○ Select what you want to appear in the chart (for the present example, select the two mean values (63.9667 and 82.5000).

Report

Mean

C Community Type	AA Academic Ability
.00 Urban	63.9667
1.00 Rural	82.5000
Total	71.3800

Figure 6.5

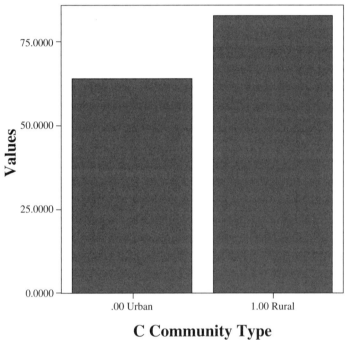

C Community Type

Figure 6.6 Interactive Chart Created From Pivot Table

○ Right-click within the selected area and choose **Create Graph, Bar.**

You will obtain the interactive graph shown in Figure 6.6.

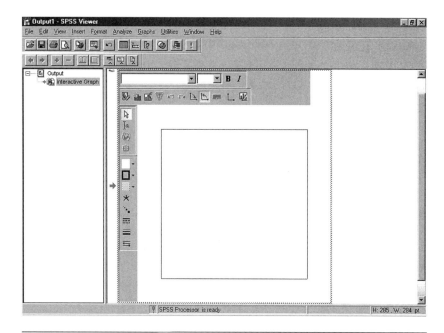

Figure 6.7 Blank Interactive Chart Inserted in Output Viewer

INSERTING CHARTS IN THE OUTPUT VIEWER

Now let's examine how you can insert a blank chart into the Output Viewer. To recreate the present example in this way,

○ Select **Insert, Interactive 2-D Graph** from the pull-down menus.

The blank graph shown in Figure 6.7 will be inserted in the viewer. Now

○ Click the "Assign Variables" icon to obtain the "Assign Variables" dialog box.

○ Drag the variable "aa" to the *y*-axis and the variable "c" to the *x*-axis, as before.

Notice that as soon as you make a change in the dialog box, that change is reflected in the graph in the viewer. Close the "Assign

Variables" dialog box and you will see that the variables have been assigned to the axes but there is no chart element. To add a chart element,

❍ Click the "Insert Element" icon and then select "Bar."

Notice that the bars are immediately added to the chart. The interactive chart provides you with the ability to change the orientation of the chart and to change whether it is a two- or three-dimensional chart by clicking the appropriate icons. You can add text anywhere in the chart by clicking the "Text Tool" icon (and return to a pointer by clicking the "Arrow Tool" icon). The chart also provides you with icons that allow you to choose fill color, border color, fill style, symbol style and size, line style and weight, and connector style. Essentially, it is as if SPSS has provided you with the Output Viewer equivalent of a pencil, paper, and eraser so that you can interactively sketch the chart of your choice.

MODIFYING CHARTS

The interactive chart feature provides you with a great deal of flexibility to modify charts either as you are making them or after they have been created. There are three primary ways to access your options for modifying charts. First, you can double-click a chart in the Output Viewer to activate it and then click the "Display the Chart Manager" icon. The Chart Manager will appear, as shown in Figure 6.8. The Chart Manager allows you to work with each of the components within the chart.

You can also access chart modification options by right-clicking on a chart element. Finally, you can also access chart modification options by double-clicking on a chart element. I encourage you to explore each of these methods for modifying charts so that you discover the many ways in which you can customize an interactive chart to your liking.

CHARTLOOKS

ChartLooks is similar to TableLooks, which was described in the previous chapter. ChartLooks consists of a collection of chart properties that may be applied in their entirety to a chart. SPSS provides you with a set of ChartLooks from which you may choose different appearances as

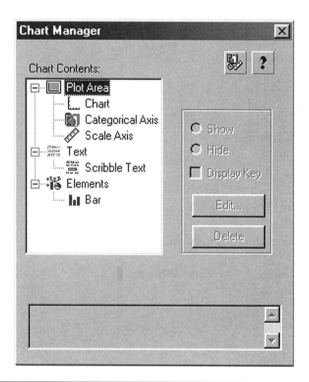

Figure 6.8 Chart Manager Dialog Box

well as with the ability to create your own ChartLooks. To apply a ChartLook to an interactive chart,

○ Double-click the chart to activate it.

○ Select **Format, ChartLooks . . .** from the pull-down menus.

○ Select the ChartLook you wish for the chart from the "ChartLooks" dialog box.

○ Click the "Apply" button.

Notice that the new properties are applied to the chart. Click the "Close" button to close the dialog box.

One way to create a custom ChartLook is to

❍   Open the "ChartLooks" dialog box.

❍   Select a ChartLook that is similar to what you desire.

❍   Click the "Edit Look" button.

❍   Modify the properties you wish to change.

❍   Click the "OK" button when you are done making your modifications.

❍   Click the "Save As" button to save the new look under a different name from the one with which you started.

Another way to create a custom ChartLook is to

❍   Create an interactive graph and modify it so that is has the look that you wish.

❍   Activate the graph.

❍   Select **Format, ChartLook . . .** from the pull-down menus.

❍   Select "Current Chart Properties" from the list of looks.

❍   Click the "Save As" button.

❍   Save the ChartLook with your desired filename (note that ChartLook files end with the .clo extension).

You can also select the ChartLook you wish to have as your default.

❍   From the Output Viewer pull-down menus, select **Edit, Options . . . .**

❍   Select the "Interactive" tab.

❍   Pick your desired default ChartLook.

❍   Click the "OK" button.

EXERCISE SEVEN

Open the Wintergreen data set. From the pull-down menus, create an interactive vertical bar chart that displays the mean parent education for males and females. Pick the bar style that is rectangular in shape. Do not display error bars. Title the chart "Wintergreen Data (Lewis-Beck, 1995)" and subtitle the chart "Mean Parent Education by Gender." Apply the Steel ChartLook. Create the chart.

EXERCISE EIGHT

Use the pull-down menus to repeat the analysis in the previous exercise. Create the same interactive chart directly from the resulting pivot table.

CHAPTER 7

Using the SPSS Production Facility

Chapter Purpose

This chapter provides readers with an understanding of the SPSS production facility.

Chapter Goal

To provide readers with skills for using the production facility.

Expectation of Readers

Readers will be able to make the most use of this chapter if they are familiar with writing and running SPSS syntax to perform data analysis. Readers are expected to write the syntax illustrated in the chapter and run it using the production facility.

INTRODUCTION

The SPSS production facility allows users to run SPSS programs unattended so that they can do other things while SPSS is running. The production facility is particularly useful for running time-consuming analyses and reporting that are done on a recurring basis. For example, you may have to run the same set of reports every quarter and the only thing that changes is the data set being analyzed. To use the production facility, you write and debug your program (or set of programs) and then submit them to the production facility to run. If you wish, you can instruct the production facility to prompt the user for input as the production job is run. There are many options available in the production facility that control how production jobs are run and the output they produce. This chapter will lead you to an understanding of the production facility.

The first step in working with the production facility is to write an SPSS syntax file containing the code you wish to run. You may use any text editor, including the SPSS Syntax window, to write your code. Let's write the following program to read the Wintergreen data, compute descriptive statistics for the "academic ability" and "parent education" variables, and compute frequency distributions for the "advisor evaluation," "student motivation," "religious affiliation," "gender," and "community type" variables (be sure to use the full path name for your data set):

```
1)  * Read Wintergreen data.
2)  * Descriptives for academic ability and parent education.
3)  * Frequencies for student motivation, advisor evaluation,
4)  * religious affiliation, gender, and community type.
5)  get file = 'Wintergreen.sav.'
6)  descriptives variables = aa pe/
7)      statistics = mean stddev min max.
8)      freq var = ae sm r g c/
9)      barchart.
```

Save the file as 'WintergreenDescFreq.sps' and close SPSS if you have it running. Now let's run the production job.

○ Run the SPSS production facility from your computer's Start menu.

○ Enter your name as the "Creator/owner."

○ Click the "Add" button, browse until you find the file 'WintergreenDescFreq.sps,' and then double-click the filename to include it in the list of syntax files.

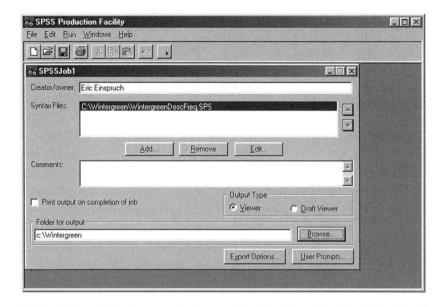

Figure 7.1 Production Facility Dialog Box

○ Browse and select the folder in which you would like the output to be saved.

The dialog box will now look like Figure 7.1.

Save the production job as 'WintergreenProdJob1.spp' using either the pull-down menus or the "Save" icon. Note that production job names end with the ".spp" extension. Once saved, run the production job as follows:

Chapter Glossary

Production facility: An SPSS feature that allows users to run SPSS programs unattended.

Production job macro: A macro that prompts the user for input as the production job is run.

○ Select **Run, Production Job** from the pull-down menus (or click the "Run" icon).

The production job will hide in the background and run the job (if you wish, you may select **Edit, Options . . .** and instruct the production facility to show SPSS when it is running).

The production job creates an output document that has the same name as the job but that ends with the ".spo" extension. To see the output document,

○ Run SPSS from the "Start" menu.

○ Open the file called 'WintergreenProdJob1.spo.'

In it, you will see a number of comments regarding the running of the production job, followed by the output from the analyses.

Let's look at how the production facility handles more than one syntax file and how it exports text and charts. First, write a second syntax file with the following codes and save it as 'WintergreenCross.sps':

```
1) *
2) * Read Wintergreen data.
3) * Crosstabs for gender by advisor evaluation.
4) get file = 'Wintergreen.sav.'
5) crosstabs tables = g by ae/
6)    cells = count row/
7)    statistics = chisq/
8)    barchart.
```

To add this file to the production job,

○ In the "Production Job" dialog box, click the "Add" button.

○ Browse until you find this file.

○ Double-click the filename to add it to the list of syntax files.

○ Click the **Export Options . . .** button and choose to export the output document (your other choices include exporting the output document without the charts, exporting the charts only, and exporting nothing).

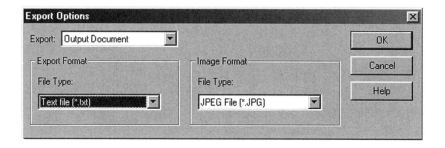

Figure 7.2 Production Facility Export Options Dialog Box

○ Select **Text File** as the file type for the export and select **JPEG File** as the file type for the image format (note that you have other options for the export and image formats).

The dialog box will now look as shown in Figure 7.2.

Run the production job again and look at the results. Perhaps the easiest way to see what the production job has done is to use the Windows Explorer to look at the files. You will note that the production job has produced an output document ('WintergreenProdJob1.spo.'), a text file export of the results ('WintergreenProdJob1.txt'), and six chart export files in JPEG format (each named sequentially beginning with 'WintergreenProdJob11.jpg.' The exported file and charts are now ready for use in other programs of your choice (go ahead and open them individually and take a look at them). If you open the output document with SPSS, you will see that the production facility ran both syntax files so that you have results for all three of the analyses (descriptives, frequencies, and crosstabs); similarly, six charts were exported because that is the number produced by the two programs.

Now let's look at how the production facility can prompt the user for input. Let's assume that the Wintergreen study is repeated annually (we might name the data sets 'Wintergreen01.sav' for year 2001, 'Wintergreen02.sav' for year 2002, and so on). Let's also assume that the same analyses are to be run each year but allow the user to select different analyses if desired. Last, let's assume that the user will appreciate having default run options to make the job easier to run and to remind them of the data set and variable naming conventions. We will write a new production job to perform these tasks.

First, modify the file that performs the descriptives and frequencies analyses so that it includes macro prompts rather than the filename and variable lists. Each macro name must begin with the "@" character and must not be more than eight characters long (note that this is necessary in the production facility but was not necessary when we were writing macros in SPSS syntax as covered in Chapter 4). The revised program looks like the following (save this file as 'WintergreenDescFreqPrompt.sps'):

```
 1) *
 2) * Read Wintergreen data.
 3) * Descriptives for academic ability and parent education.
 4) * Frequencies for student motivation, advisor evaluation,
 5) * religious affiliation, gender, and community type.
 6) get file = @data.
 7) descriptives variables = @descvar /
 8)    statistics = mean stddev min max.
 9)    freq var = @freqvar/
10)    barchart.
```

Similarly, modify the file that performs the cross-tabulation analysis so that it includes macro prompts rather than the filename and variable lists. Because this program will read the same data set, use the same macro name to specify the data to be read. The revised program looks like the following (save this file as 'WintergreenCross Prompt.sps'):

```
1) *
2) * Read Wintergreen data.
3) * Crosstabs for gender by advisor evaluation.
4) get file = @data.
5) crosstabs tables = @crosvar/
6)    cells = count row/
7)    statistics = chisq/
8)    barchart.
```

Also, make a copy of the Wintergreen data set and name it 'Wintergreen01.sav.'

To add these files to a production job,

○ Close any other production jobs you have open.

○ From the menu, select **File, New.**

○ Enter your name for the "Creator/owner."

○ Click the "Add" button, browse until you find the two files we just created, and double-click them to add them to the production job.

○ Add any comments you wish in the "Comments" box.

○ Browse and select a folder for the output and select any export options you wish.

Now click the "User Prompts" button and you will see its dialog box. You will work with the data file macro in the first row.

○ Enter "@data" for the macro symbol.

○ Enter "Data file for analysis" for the prompt.

○ Enter 'Wintergreen01.sav' for the default (be sure you use the full path name for your data set).

○ Enter "Yes" in the last column because data filenames need to be enclosed in quotes.

In the second row of the dialog box, you will work with the macro for the list of variables to be analyzed by the `descriptives` procedure.

○ Enter "@descvar" for the macro symbol.

○ Enter "Variables for the descriptives analysis" for the prompt.

○ Enter "aa pe" for the default.

○ Enter "No" in the last column because variable names do not need to be enclosed in quotes in this case.

Now complete the third row of the dialog box to work with the macro for the list to be analyzed by the `frequencies` procedure.

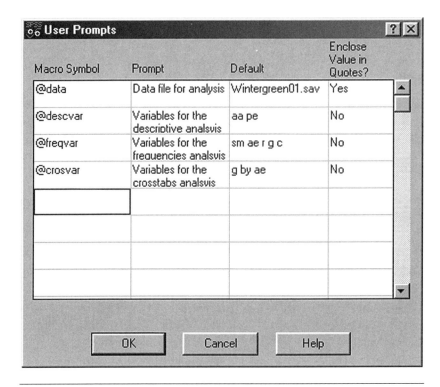

Figure 7.3 Production Facility User Options Dialog Box

○ Enter "@freqvar" for the macro symbol.

○ Enter "Variables for the frequencies analysis" for the prompt.

○ Enter "ae sm r g c" for the default.

○ Enter "No" in the last column because variable names do not need to be enclosed in quotes in this case.

Finally, complete the fourth row of the dialog box to work with the macro for the table for crosstabs to analyze as follows:

○ Enter "@crosvar" for the macro symbol.

○ Enter "Variables for the crosstabs analysis" for the prompt.

○ Enter "g by ae" for the default.

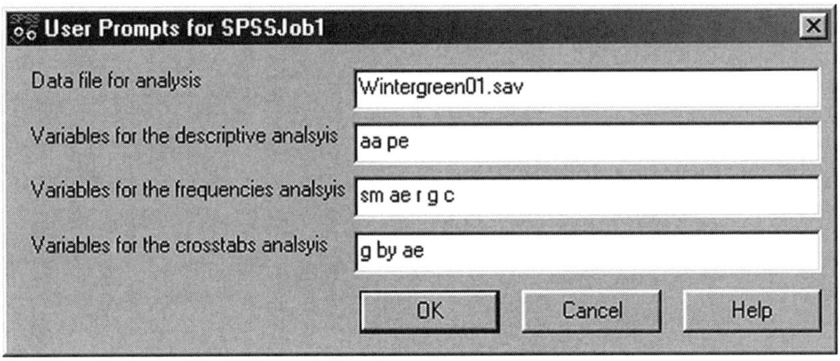

Figure 7.4 Production Facility User Prompts Dialog Box

○ Enter "No" in the last column because variable names do not need to be enclosed in quotes in this case.

Your completed "User Prompt" dialog box will look like Figure 7.3.

○ Click the "OK" button to close the dialog box.

○ From the menu, select **File, Save As . . .** and then save the job as 'WintergreenProdJobPrompt.spp.'

○ Run the production job.

The production facility will prompt you with the dialog box found in Figure 7.4.

This dialog box prompts you for the information you wish to use for the data filename and variable list macros. It also provides you with the default values. Notice how easy it would be to change any of these values, for example, to change 'Wintergreen01.sav' to 'Wintergreen02.sav' to analyze a different year's data.

Click "OK" to accept the default values, which are passed to all the syntax files in the production job for use by the macros that need them.

Once the production job is completed, use SPSS to open the 'WintergreenProdJobPrompt.spo' file to see the results of the job. In particular, examine the log at the beginning of the file to see how the production job has resolved the macro definitions and included the syntax files.

EXERCISE NINE

Use the SPSS production facility to run the syntax file created in Exercise 1.

EXERCISE TEN

Rewrite the syntax file created in Exercise 1 so that the two factors analyzed by the ANOVA are represented by macro prompts, and save the file as 'Norpoth2.sps.' Use the SPSS production facility to write a production job that prompts the user for the factors, and then run the syntax file and save the production job as 'Norpoth2.spp.'

▓ CHAPTER 8

Using the SPSS Scripting Facility

Chapter Purpose

This chapter introduces readers to the vast world of SPSS scripting.

Chapter Goal

To provide readers with fundamental skills for writing SPSS scripts.

Expectation of Readers

Readers will be able to make the most use of this chapter if they are comfortable writing and running SPSS syntax, are comfortable studying SPSS syntax to discern its meaning, and are facile at relating SPSS output to the syntax that produced it. Readers are expected to use abstract-thinking skills to conceptualize how scripts work. Readers are expected to write and run the SPSS code that is presented in the chapter so that they see the results of the operations.

INTRODUCTION

The SPSS scripting facility is a remarkable tool you can use to automate SPSS tasks. For example, you can automatically customize output in the SPSS Viewer, open and save data files, display and manipulate dialog

G Gender * SM Student Motivation Cross Tabulation

			SM Student Motivation			
			.00 Not Willing	1.00 Undecided	2.00 Willing	Total
G Gender	.00 Male	Count	9	13	6	28
		% within G Gender	32.1%	46.4%	21.4%	100.0%
	1.00 Female	Count	4	10	8	22
		% within G Gender	18.2%	45.5%	36.4%	100.0%
Total		Count	13	23	14	50
		% within G Gender	26.0%	46.0%	28.0%	100.0%

Figure 8.1   Cross-Tabulation of Gender by Student Motivation

boxes, run data transformations and statistical procedures using SPSS syntax, and export charts as graphic files in a variety of formats. This chapter covers the fundamentals of the scripting facility. It also directs you to resources for learning more about scripts, as there is a wealth of information available to you. The SPSS scripting facility gives you a great deal of control over SPSS, much as running procedures from syntax gives you far more control and options than running procedures from pull-down menus. In this chapter, we will run a script, think about how scripts work, write scripts, look at debugging scripts, create an autoscript, and run a script from syntax.

RUNNING A SCRIPT

Let's start by running the script that came with your SPSS program that reformats pivot tables to make a row or column labeled "total" so that the results they contain are made bold and colored blue. First, open the Wintergreen data file and run a `crosstab` analysis with gender in the rows and student motivation in the columns and request row percentages in the cells and a chi-square test of significance. Run the analysis from either the pull-down menus or the Syntax window. Your output will look like Figure 8.1.

To run the script,

❍ Click on the "gender by student motivation cross-tabulation" pivot table to select it.

○ Select **Utilities, Run Script . . .** from the pull-down menus. SPSS will present you with several scripts that came with your program (you can find them in the ' . . . \spss\scripts' directory).

○ Click the file called 'Make totals bold.sbs.'

○ Select the **Run** button.

Notice that SPSS has reformatted the selected pivot table according to the instructions in the script; that is, the results in the row and column labeled "total" are now bold and blue.

AUTOSCRIPTS

Autoscripts run automatically when a particular procedure creates a particular output. From the menu, you can select **Edit, Options . . . Scripts** to see the autoscripts that SPSS has provided for you (see Figure 8.2). Simply check the autoscripts that you wish to enable.

For example, one of the autoscripts available to you is called 'Correlations_Table_Correlations_Create.sbs.' This autoscript removes the upper diagonal from a correlation matrix and highlights significant correlations. This autoscript saves you from having to make these changes to the correlation pivot table using your mouse or by running a particular script. To see the effect of the autoscript,

---

Chapter Glossary

Autoscript: A script that runs automatically, triggered when a given procedure creates a specific piece of output.

Methods: Actions that can be performed on an object (e.g., selecting all elements in a table).

Properties: Characteristics of an object (e.g., the font of the text in a table).

Script: SPSS commands that use methods and properties to act on objects.

Starter scripts: Scripts provided by SPSS that supply code for one or more common procedures, commented with hints on how to customize the script to the user's particular needs.

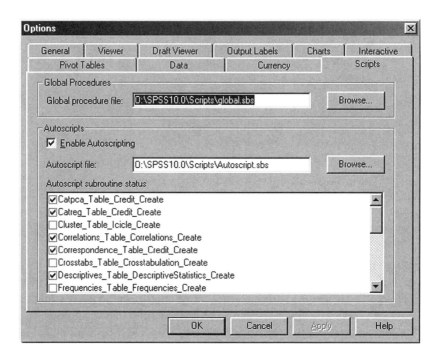

Figure 8.2 Script Options Dialog Box

○ Open the Wintergreen data set.

○ Run a correlation between "academic ability" and "parent education."

The correlation table is shown in Figure 8.3.

○ From the menu, select **Edit, Options . . . Scripts.**

○ Enable the autoscripts called 'Correlations_Table_Correlations_ Create.sbs.'

○ Rerun the correlation analysis.

The correlation table now looks as shown in Figure 8.4.

You can create your own autoscript, which will be stored in the autoscript file (all autoscripts are stored in a single file rather than in separate files like other scripts are), by doing the following:

Correlations

		AA Academic Ability	PE Parents' Education
AA Academic Ability	Pearson Correlation	1.000	.793**
	Sig. (2-tailed)	.	.000
	N	50	50
PE Parents' Education	Pearson Correlation	.793**	1.000
	Sig. (2-tailed)	.000	.
	N	50	50

**. Correlation is significant at the 0.01 level (2-tailed).

Figure 8.3 Output From Correlations Procedure

Correlations

		AA Academic Ability	PE Parents' Education
AA Academic Ability	Pearson Correlation		
	Sig. (2-tailed)		
	N		
PE Parents' Education	Pearson Correlation	.793**	
	Sig. (2-tailed)	.000	
	N	50	

**. Correlation is significant at the 0.01 level (2-tailed).

Figure 8.4 Output From Correlations Procedure After Running Script

❍ Go to an output document.

❍ Select the object you want to trigger the autoscript by single-clicking it.

❍ From the menu, select **Utilities, Create/Edit Autoscript** (you can also get this choice using the right mouse button). The Script Editor window will appear, and it will either be ready for you to enter a new script if one does not already exist or it will show you the existing script if there already is one.

❍ Enter your code for the script.

❍ From the menu, choose **Edit, Options** to enable or disable the autoscript.

The autoscript will be named according to the procedure that triggers it. For example, if you create an autoscript that is run when the `fre-quencies` procedure creates a frequencies table, the name of the auto-script will be "Frequencies_Table_Frequencies_Create."

THINKING ABOUT HOW SCRIPTS WORK

In thinking about how scripts work, let's start by considering the day-to-day life example of using a pencil at home. For me to actually use my pencil, I have to go through several steps. Although I can be as general or as detailed as I wish in my description of the steps I have to go through, let me describe the actions as follows. First, I have to be in my home. Next, I have to go into my study, which is the particular room in my home where the pencil is. There are several items in my study, among them my desk. I go to my desk and open the desk drawer, which contains many items itself, including several different kinds of pencils (regular wood pencil, mechanical pencil, and art pencils of different colors). I then get the pencil I want and use it to write and erase.

To carry this analogy to SPSS, let's think about changing the "Title" line in the SPSS output that displays the results of the cross-tabulation we did in the preceding section. First, I start the SPSS software (i.e., the SPSS "application"). Then I open the Wintergreen data file and run the `crosstab` analysis (with gender in the rows and student motivation in the columns, row percentages in the cells, and a chi-square test of significance). Next, I go to the Output Document window (rather than, say, the Data Editor or the Syntax window; each of these windows is known by SPSS script as a "document"). In the left pane of the window, I see the collection of "output items" in the output document and I click on the one "output item" that I wish, in this case, the one marked "Title" (had I chosen, I could have gotten one of the other output items such as the "Notes," "Case processing summary," "Gender by student motivation cross-tabulation," or "Chi-square tests"). This "gets" the title in the right pane, which at present says "Crosstabs," and I can now do things *with* the title such as copy it. If I go to the right-hand pane and "activate" the title by double-clicking it, I can then do things *to* the title itself, such as change it to something like "My new title." At this point, you should

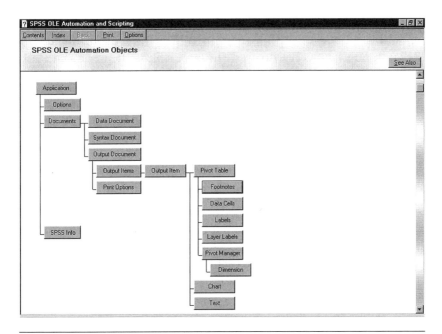

Figure 8.5 Tree View of Object Hierarchy

actually perform these steps on your computer to get the best sense for this sequence of steps.

The way one navigates through the SPSS "objects" is illustrated in Figure 8.5. Work your way from left to right through this illustration to follow the present example. I launched SPSS (i.e., the application) and ran the analysis, which involved at least two documents (the data document and the output document; if you ran the analysis from the Syntax window, then a syntax document was also involved). Next, I selected the output document with its collection of output items, including the collection of objects associated with the crosstabs analysis. Last, I selected the title, which is a "Text" object.

Whenever you write a script, you always have to start with the highest level in the outline (known as the "object hierarchy") and work your way down to the level on which you wish to operate, just as I did when I went into my home to get a pencil. Each object, in the real world of my home and in the world of SPSS, has "features" and "uses." The pencils in my desk have features such as their color and how hard they are and uses such as writing and erasing. The title in the `crosstab` output is a text object that has the feature of the text itself (that is, "Cross-tabulation" or "My new title"), but it has no uses. The pivot table in the `crosstab` output has many features (such as background color and text font) and many uses (such as select all footnotes and hide footnotes). When programmers speak, they refer to features as "properties" and uses as "methods."

WRITING SCRIPTS

Now let's write a simple script that deletes the titles in the open output document and inserts one new title. The script assumes that you are running SPSS and that there is an open output document with results in it (be sure this is the case before attempting to run the script—you can recreate the cross-tabulation above if you wish). This example illustrates several important points about writing scripts, although you will quickly want to expand it to be more versatile.

○ From the menu, select **File, New, Script.** You will be presented with the Script Editor window and the "Use Starter Script" dialog box.

○ Click the "Cancel" button to close the dialog box.

The Script Editor window will appear as in Figure 8.6.

Now enter the following code between "Sub Main" and "End Sub" in the Script Editor window:

```
1) 'Delete output document titles and insert a new title'
2) Dim objOutputDoc As ISpssOutputDoc
3) Dim objOutputItems As ISpssItems
4) Dim strLabel As String
5) Dim strTitleText As String
6) strLabel = "New Label"
7) strTitleText = "New Title"
8) Set objOutputDoc = objSpssApp.GetDesignatedOutputDoc
9) Set objOutputItems = objOutputDoc.Items
10) objOutputDoc.SelectAllTitles
11) objOutputDoc.Remove
12) objOutputDoc.InsertTitle (strLabel, strTitleText)
```

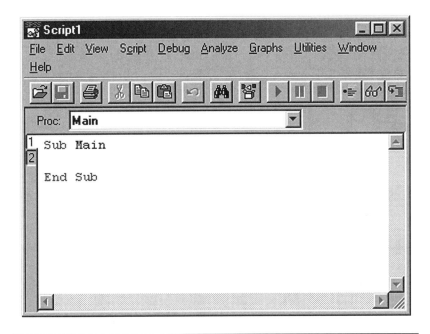

Figure 8.6 Script Editor Window

Let's take a close look at this script and see how it works. All scripts must have at least one subroutine, like the one we have here that begins with "Sub Main" and ends with "End Sub." The code appears in different colors in the Script Editor window: In general, comments are displayed in green, reserved words are displayed in blue, and objects, properties, and methods are displayed in magenta. Line 1 of the script is a comment because it starts with the single quotation mark, and it is displayed in green. It is a good idea to always comment your syntax and script code liberally.

Next, we create the variables we are going to use in the script and indicate what type of variables they are. The act of creating the variable is referred to as "declaring" them, and this is done with the "Dim" statement. Thus, line 2 states "Dim objOutputDoc As ISpssOutputDoc" and creates a variable called "objOutputDoc" that represents SPSS output documents. Similarly, line 3 states "Dim objOutputItems As ISpssItems" and creates a variable called "objOutputDoc" that represents the items that are collected within an SPSS output document. Lines 4 and 5 create two other variables, "strLabel" and "strTitleText," both of which are string variables that can take on character values. You can name your variables anything you wish, but convention suggests that you begin your variable names by indicating what kind of variable it is. Thus, "strLabel" could have simply been called "Label," but by adding the "str" at the beginning of the name, we are always reminded that it is a string variable.

Once the variables have been declared (i.e., now that they exist), we can do things with them. First, we assign values to the string variables. In line 6, "strLabel" is assigned the value "New Label," and in line 7, "strTitleText" is assigned the value "New Title." We then use set to get the items that we want. The set in line 8 uses a method that belongs to the SPSS application, which is the highest object in the hierarchy (see Figure 8.2). Remember, you use objects higher in the hierarchy to get objects that are lower. The set in line 9 assigns the output document items to the variable "objOutputItems."

The last three lines of code use methods that belong to the output document. Line 10 selects all the titles, line 11 deletes them, and line 12 inserts a new title. The value of the variable "strLabel" (in our case, "New Label") will appear in the left pane of the Output Document window, and the value of the variable "strTitleText" (in our case, "New Title") will appear as the new title in the right pane of the window.

❍   Save this script as 'RemoveAndInsertTitle.sbs.' Note that scripts end with the suffix "sbs."

❍   Run the script from within the Script Editor window by selecting **Script, Run** from the pull-down menus or by clicking the "Run" icon on the toolbar.

❍   Study the Output Document window to see how it has been modified by the script.

In the left-hand pane, you will see that the item that used to be read "Title" now reads "New Label," and in the right-hand pane, you will see that the item that used to be labeled "Crosstabs" is now labeled "New Title."

Now let's take a look at a second example. This is a slightly edited version of an example that appears in the **Help** menu available in the Script Editor window (it also appears in the *SPSS 10.0 Developer's Guide*). The purpose of this script is to find output titles that say "Crosstabs" and change them so they say "My new title for crosstabs."

```
 1) Sub Main
 2)      'Declare variables'
 3)      Dim objOutputDoc As ISpssOutputDoc
 4)      Dim objOutputItems As ISpssItems
 5)      Dim objOutputItem As ISpssItem
 6)      Dim objSPSSText As ISpssrtf
 7)      Dim intItemCount As Integer 'Number of output items'
 8)      Dim intItemType As Integer 'Output item type'
 9)      Dim strItemTitle As String 'Text to find and change'
10)      'Get the viewer window and output items'
11)      Set objOutputDoc = objSpssApp.GetDesignatedOutputDoc
12)      Set objOutputItems=objOutputDoc.Items()
13)      'Loop through output items to find matching type and text'
14)      'If crosstabs, then change'
15)      intItemCount = objOutputItems.Count
16)      For Index = 0 To intItemCount-1
17)          Set objOutputItem=objOutputItems.GetItem(Index)
18)          intItemType = objOutputItem.SPSSType
19)          If intItemType = SPSSTitle Then
20)              Set objSPSSText = objOutputItem.Activate
21)              strItemTitle = objSPSSText.Text
22)              If strItemTitle = "Crosstabs" Then
23)                 objSPSSText.Text = "My new title for crosstabs"
24)                    objOutputItem.Deactivate
25)                    Exit For
26)              End If
27)          End If
28)      Next
29) End Sub
```

Go ahead and type this script into the Script Editor window and then save it as 'MyNewTitleForCrosstabs.sbs.'

Let's examine this script closely. As you know, every script must have at least one subroutine. This script has only one subroutine and it is defined by "Sub Main" in line 1 and "End Sub" in line 29. Line 2 is a comment that tells you that the variables are about to be declared and is followed by the declarations themselves in lines 3–9. Each variable is also assigned a type; thus, "objOutputDoc" can be an SPSS output document, "objOutputItems" can be the collection of output items in an output document, "objOutputItem" can be an item within the collection of output items, "objSPSSText" can be a text object, "intItemCount" and "intItemType" can be integers (note that their names begin with "int" to reflect that they are of the integer type), and "strItemTitle" can be a string (note that its name begins with "str" to reflect that it is of the string type). The comments in the declarations inform you a bit about how the integer and string variables will be used.

In lines 10–12, the script gets the currently designated output document by using the SPSS application method "GetDesignatedOutputDoc" and assigns it to the variable "objOutputDoc." The items within the output document are then assigned to the variable "objOutputItems." The script then looks through the collection of output items until it finds a title that says "Crosstabs." First, in line 15, the variable "intItemCount" is assigned the value that represents the number of output items that there are (using the "Count" method that belongs to the output items). In line 16, the script then sets up a loop that runs as many times as there are items (the loop starts at 0 and ends at one less than the number of items because that's the way they are counted by the program). In line 17, the script gets the output item indexed by the loop using the "GetItem" method that belongs to output items. Thus, the first time through the loop, the index is set to 0 and the script gets the first output item; the second time through, the index is set to 1 and the script gets the second output item; and so on. In line 18, the variable "intItemType" is assigned the type of the output item that the script just got. If the output item is a title (line 19), then it is activated in line 20 (just like you activate it in the Output window if you double-click on it), and in line 21, the variable "strItemTitle" is assigned the text in the title. If this text says "Crosstabs" (line 22), then the text is replaced with "My new title for crosstabs" (line 23), and the object is then deactivated in line 24 (just like you deactivate text in the Output window by clicking outside the object). The "Exit For" in line 25 closes the loop, and then there is one "End If" statement for every previous "If" statement ("If" in line 19 and "End If" in line 27; "If" in line 22 and "End If" in line 26). The "Next" in line 28 closes the loop begun in line 16. Finally, the subroutine ends in line 29.

Now let's run the script as follows:

○ Open the 'Wintergreen.sav' data file.

○ Run a frequency distribution on the "community type" variable.

❍ Run a cross-tabulation with "gender" in the rows and "advisor evaluation" in the columns and row percentages in the cells.

Once the analyses have been completed, examine the Output Document window and look at the titles for the two analyses. Notice that the first title is "Frequencies" and the second title is "Crosstabs."

❍ Run the 'MyNewTextForCrosstabs.sbs' script.

Examine the Output Document window to see that the title for the frequency distribution is still "Frequencies" but the title for the cross-tabulation has changed to "My new title for crosstabs."

Just as debugging is part of the fun with writing SPSS syntax, so it is also part of the fun of writing SPSS script. Do not worry; SPSS will tell you if your script does not execute properly. The script will stop running, the line that has caused an error will be highlighted in red, and SPSS will give you an indication of the problem. You can correct your mistake based on this information and rerun your script to see if you have corrected the problem. You will go through this cycle as many times as necessary to eliminate the errors. Do not be discouraged, as all programmers debug their code because it is rare that code is perfect when it is first written. However, starter scripts may help you minimize errors when you are first beginning to write scripts (starter scripts are discussed in the next section).

You can also use the Script Editor's debugging pull-down menu to get information about the status of the script as it is running. You will likely want to begin using this feature once you become familiar with writing and running scripts.

USING STARTER SCRIPTS

SPSS has been kind to you by providing several "starter scripts." These scripts are designed for you to use as you develop your own scripts. They are generally quite flexible and provide you with a considerable amount of code that you can often edit so that it accomplishes your particular purpose. These starter scripts are also very instructive to study and will help you learn about objects, properties, methods, and writing scripts. I encourage you to make good use of these starter scripts.

Of course, any existing script can be used as a starter script. As an example, the script you just wrote can be edited to change the title of a frequency distribution instead of a cross-tabulation. Simply change the line that states

```
If strItemTitle = "Crosstabs" Then
objSPSSText.Text = "My new title for crosstabs"
```

to

```
If strItemTitle = "Frequencies" Then
objSPSSText.Text = "My new title for frequencies"
```

and save the script as 'MyNewTitleForFrequencies.sbs' and you will have used one script to help you write another.

Let's look at one of the starter scripts provided by SPSS.

○ From the menu, select **File, New, Script.**

○ Select 'Delete Navigator Items.sbs' from the "Use Starter Script" dialog box.

Notice that the lines of code from the starter script have been inserted into the Script Editor window rather than the starter script itself having been opened. When you save your new script, you will be prompted for a filename and will create a new file rather than saving over the original starter script file.

The 'Delete Navigator Items.sbs' script has been written to delete the output document items that you select. You can also specify conditions under which they will be deleted. All of the lines that cause an action have been commented out, and you simply remove the single quotation mark before those lines that perform the action you wish to perform. The script is nicely documented with comments, and you will learn a great deal by studying the comments and following how the script works. For now, simply open an output document that contains the results of a few analyses (or open a data file and run a few analyses so that they appear in the output document). Then run the script and review the output document. You will notice that nothing has happened because all the lines that cause action have been commented out.

Now, let's go ahead and remove all the "Notes" from the output document. In the script, remove the single quotation mark from the beginning of the 28th line so that it reads

```
intTypeToDelete = SPSSNote
```

Also, remove the single quotation mark from the beginning of the 44th line so that it reads

```
Call DeleteAllByType(intTypeToDelete)
```

Now run the script and examine the output document. You will notice that the "Notes" are no longer there. Such a simple modification to a fairly complicated file that has already been written for you! Spend some time studying this starter file to see what else it can do for you. Now save your new script with the name 'RemoveAllNotes.sbs.' The next time you wish to use it, you can simply

○ Select **Utilities, Run Script . . .** from the menu.

○ Double-click on this filename (of course, you may need to browse to find the file, depending on where you have saved it).

RUNNING A SCRIPT FROM SYNTAX

You can run a script from within your syntax program by using the `script` command. Simply write the command followed by the script you wish to run. As an example, write and run the following code to open the Wintergreen data set, create a cross-tabulation of gender by student motivation, calculate a chi-square test of significance, and run the script you wrote and saved earlier that changes the title from "Crosstabs" to "My new title for crosstabs" (be sure to include the full path name for your data set and script file):

```
1) *.
2) * This code illustrates running a script from within syntax
3) *.
4) get file = 'Wintergreen.sav.'
5) crosstabs tables = g by sm/
6)    cells = count row/
7)    statistics = chisq.
8) script file = 'MyNewTitleForCrosstabs.sbs.'
```

Lines 1–3 provide comments for this code. Line 4 reads the Wintergreen data set, and lines 5–7 create the cross-tabulation. Line 8 of the code runs the named script file. You can also pass a parameter from syntax to the script. First, declare a variable in your script that will accept the parameter. For example, to pass a string parameter, declare the variable as a string as follows:

```
Dim strParam as String
```

Next, in your script, assign this variable the value of the parameter when it is passed from syntax to the script.

```
set strParam = objSPSSApp.ScriptParameter (0)
```

Finally, include the parameter in the syntax line that runs the script as

```
script file = 'name of script file' ('Parameter').
```

GETTING HELP

There are several sources of information that can help you learn about writing SPSS script. One is the *SPSS Base 10.0 User's Guide.* Another is the help menu you access from the Script Editor window. In particular, in the Script Editor window, the pull-down menus **Help, SPSS Objects** bring you to the illustration of the object hierarchy that is shown in Figure 8.2. You can then click on any of the object types to learn more about that type and its associated properties and methods. You can also select **Debug, Object Browser** from the Script Editor window pull-down menus to explore the available object classes and the methods and properties associated with them (see Figure 8.7).

In addition, you can visit the "Script Exchange" page on SPSS's World Wide Web site (http://spss.com/tech/scptxchg/). Use these sources of information as you study and use the scripts that SPSS has provided you as you create your own scripts, as they will help you become a facile script writer.

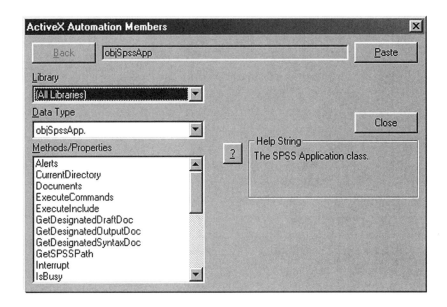

Figure 8.7 SPSS Object Browser

EXERCISE ELEVEN

Run the ANOVA in Exercise 1. Select the ANOVA table in the output. From the utilities pull-down menu, find and run the script that makes the "Total" line in the table bold. Note the effect the script has on the table.

EXERCISE TWELVE

Open the Script window. When prompted with the starter script dialog box, navigate to find the script you ran in Exercise 11. Find the line of code that turns the table text bold and comment it out. Find the line of code that turns the table text to bold italic and change it from a comment to a line of executable code. Find the line of code that turns the table text blue and comment it out. Find the line of code that turns the table text red and change it from a comment to a line of executable code. Save the script as 'MakeTotalsBoldItalicRed.sbs.' Run the script and note its effect on the table. Study the other lines of code in this script and determine the function of each line.

EXERCISE THIRTEEN

Add the script you created in Exercise 12 ('MakeTotalsBoldItalic Red.sbs') to your collection of autoscripts but do not select it. Clear the Output window and rerun the ANOVA from Exercise 1. Select the autoscript 'Make totals bold 2.sbs' and again rerun the ANOVA. Compare the two ANOVA tables you just obtained.

CHAPTER 9

Using the SPSS Matrix Command Language

Chapter Purpose

This chapter introduces readers to the SPSS matrix language.

Chapter Goal

To provide readers with fundamental skills for using the SPSS matrix language.

Expectation of Readers

Readers will be able to make the most use of this chapter if they are familiar with matrix algebra and its application in statistical analysis. Readers are expected to write and run the SPSS code that is presented in the chapter so that they see the result of the operations.

INTRODUCTION

The matrix command language is used to perform mathematical calculations using matrix algebra. It also allows you to write your own statistical routines using matrix algebra. Matrix command language skills are important for many who use advanced statistical techniques.

This chapter will introduce you to the fundamentals of the SPSS matrix command language, but it does not attempt to explain the rules of matrix algebra, which are covered in many statistics textbooks. Keep in mind as you work through this chapter that we are yet again using another language—we began by using SPSS syntax, then used macros, then wrote scripts, and will now use the matrix command language. Although all of these languages are similar in some regards, you will be most successful with these languages if you are flexible in using your knowledge of SPSS syntax as a base for understanding them.

Let's begin with an example that creates and sums two matrices.

```
 1) *
 2) * Start matrix processing
 3) *.
 4) matrix.
 5) *
 6) * Compute matrices a and b explicitly
 7) *.
 8) compute a = {1,2;3,4}.
 9) compute b = {5,6;7,8}.
10) *
11) * Add a plus b
12) *.
13) compute c = a + b.
14) *
15) * Print results
16) *.
17) print a/
18)    title = 'Matrix A.'
19) print b/
20)    title = 'Matrix B.'
21) print c/
22)    title = 'Matrix C.'
23) *
24) * End matrix processing
25) *.
26) end matrix.
```

Lines 1–4 instruct SPSS that the commands following line 4 (and up to the end matrix command in line 26) are to be executed using the SPSS matrix processor. Lines 5–9 create the two-by-two matrices *A* and

```
Run MATRIX procedure:

Matrix A
   1   2
   3   4

Matrix B
   5   6
   7   8

Matrix C
   6    8
  10   12


------ END MATRIX -----
```

Figure 9.1 Output From First Example Matrix Program

B, where the first row of *A* contains the values 1 and 2, the second row of *A* contains the values 3 and 4, the first row of *B* contains the values 5 and 6, and the second row of *B* contains the values 7 and 8. Lines 10–13 create matrix *C* by adding matrices *A* and *B.* Lines 14–22 print the three matrices in the SPSS Output Viewer window. Lines 23–26 instruct SPSS to leave the matrix processor and return to processing the syntax commands. Enter and run this syntax and note that the output looks like that shown in Figure 9.1.

Now let's consider the matrix language using simple regression as an illustration. This example will help you discover the possibilities within

Chapter Glossary

Matrix command language: Statements executed by the SPSS matrix processor to handle variables that represent matrices (i.e., sets of values arranged in rectangular arrays of rows and columns).

the SPSS matrix language, the power of which will be fully revealed once you apply SPSS's capabilities to more complicated problems. To generate the illustration:

○ Open the Wintergreen data file.

○ Run a simple regression analysis with parents' education as the predictor and academic ability as the criterion.

You may run the analysis using either the pull-down menus or the following syntax:

```
1)  *
2)  * This code runs a simple regression with parent's education
3)  * as the predictor and academic ability as the criterion
4)  *.
5)  regression/
6)  dependent aa/
7)     method = enter pe.
```

SPSS will return the results shown in Figure 9.2.

As you can see from these results, 63% of the variance in academic ability is accounted for by parents' education (R^2), the regression model is significant ($F[1, 48] = 81.41$, $p < .001$), the standard error of the estimate is 10.72, the intercept (constant) is not significantly different from zero but the regression coefficient is, and the regression equation is:

$$Y' = 1.659 + 5.045X$$

Now let us use the matrix command language to re-create these results. Recall that the regression coefficients can be obtained by solving the matrix expression:

$$b = (X'X)^{-1}X'Y$$

where b is a column vector of the intercept and regression coefficients, X is a matrix where the first column is all "1" and the subsequent columns contain the value of each dependent variable for each case

Model Summary

Model	R	R Square	Adjusted R Square	Std. Error of the Estimate
1	.793[a]	.629	.621	10.7173

a. Predictors: (Constant), PE Parents' education

ANOVA[b]

Model		Sum of Squares	df	Mean Square	F	Sig.
1	Regression	9350.443	1	9350.443	81.406	.000[a]
	Residual	5513.337	48	114.861		
	Total	14863.780	49			

a. Predictors: (Constant), PE Parents' education

b. Dependent Variable: AA Academic ability

Coefficients[a]

Model		Unstandardized Coefficients		Standardized Coefficients	t	Sig.
		B	Std. Error	Beta		
1	(Constant)	1.659	7.875		.211	.834
	PE Parents' education	5.045	.559	.793	9.023	.000

a. Dependent Variable: AA Academic ability

Figure 9.2

(i.e., the rows represent cases and the columns represent dependent variables, except that the first column has a value of 1 for every case so the intercept may be obtained; in the present example there is one dependent variable), and Y is a column vector with the values of the dependent variable for each case. With this in mind, we can write the following matrix command language statements in an SPSS Syntax window. The statements will be examined a few at a time; once they are all entered, you may run them to obtain the desired output, which repeats the results generated by SPSS for the example presented above.

```
1) *
2) * Start matrix processing
3) *.
4) matrix.
```

Lines 1–3 provide the first comments for this code. The matrix command language processor is started by the SPSS command `matrix` in line 4.

```
 5) *
 6) * Read the SPSS data file
 7) * Store the predictor in a matrix
 8) *.
 9) get tempx/
10)     file = 'filename'/
11)     variables = pe/
12)     names = vnames1.
```

In line 9 the matrix `get` command reads an SPSS data file and creates a matrix (in this example, the matrix is named *tempx*). Line 10 specifies the data file to be read, and you should replace *filename* with the name of the file in which you have stored the Wintergreen data. Line 11 specifies which variables are to be included in the matrix. In this example, parents' education is the only variable that has been included in the matrix *tempx*. Thus, *tempx* is a matrix with 50 rows (because there are 50 cases in the data set) and one column (*pe*), which contains the values of parents' education for each case (technically, this would be a column vector because there is only one column). Line 12 specifies a vector in which the variable names are stored (in this example, the vector has been called *vnames1*). Note that you can insert comments into a stream of matrix language commands in the same ways that you can insert them into a stream of syntax commands. Note also that SPSS can read data from a character-format file using the command `read` (instead of `get`), and it can read an SPSS matrix-format file using the command `mget`.

```
13) *
14) * Read the SPSS data file
15) * Store the criterion in a matrix
16) *.
17) get y/
```

```
18)     file = 'filename'/
19)     variables = aa/
20)     names = vnames2.
```

Lines 17–20 are similar to the ones we just examined. Again, you should replace *filename* with the name of the file in which you have stored the Wintergreen data. These commands create a matrix named *y* that contains each case's values for the variable *academic ability*. Again, this matrix is actually a column vector with 50 rows (because there are 50 cases in the data set) and one column (*aa*). The variable names are also stored in a vector (in this example, the vector has been called *vnames2*).

```
21) *
22) * Create a column vector of 1's for the intercept
23) *.
24) compute intvect = make(50,1,1).
```

Line 24 uses the matrix `compute` command to create a new variable named *intvect* (for "intercept vector"). The matrix function `make` creates a matrix whose elements all have the same value. The `make` function takes three arguments: The first specifies the number of rows, the second specifies the number of columns, and the third specifies the value of the elements. In this example, we have created a column vector with 50 rows, and each element has the value 1.

```
25) *
26) * Merge the column vector of 1's with the predictor to
27) * create matrix "X"
28) *.
29) compute x = {intvect, tempx}.
```

There are many ways you can construct a matrix in SPSS. In line 29 we have used the `compute` command to create a matrix called *x* that combines *intvect* and *tempx* (note that *intvect* and *tempx* are enclosed in braces and separated by a comma). The resulting matrix contains 50 rows (one for each case) and two columns (one for *intvect* and one for *tempx*).

```
30) *
31) * Compute regression coefficients
32) *.
33) compute xp = transpos(x).
34) compute xpx= xp * x.
35) compute xpxinv = inv(xpx).
36) compute xpy = xp * y.
37) compute b = xpxinv * xpy.
```

These commands illustrate additional matrix compute functions. Line 33 creates a variable named *xp* (for "x prime") that is the transpose of the matrix *x* (i.e., the rows have become the columns and the columns have become the rows). Line 34 creates a matrix called *xpx* by multiplying the matrix *xp* and the matrix *x* (remember that the order in which matrices are multiplied makes a difference in their product). Line 35 creates a matrix called *xpxinv* by taking the inverse of the matrix *xpx*. Line 36 creates a matrix called *xpy* by multiplying the matrix *xp* and the matrix *y*. Line 37 creates the vector *b* by multiplying the matrix *xpxinv* and the matrix *xpy*.

```
38) *
39) * Compute sums of squares
40) *.
41) compute bp = transpos(b).
42) compute bpxpy = bp * xpy.
43) compute sumy = csum(y).
44) compute sumysq = sumy**2.
45) compute sumysqn = sumysq/nrow(y).
46) compute yp = transpos(y).
47) compute ypy = yp * y.
48) compute ssreg = bpxpy-sumysqn.
49) compute ssres = ypy - bpxpy.
50) compute sstot = ssreg + ssres.
```

Lines 41–50 compute the required sums of squares: regression sum of squares, residual sum of squares, and total sum of squares. The regression sum of squares is computed first from the formula:

$$ssreg = b'X'Y - ((\Sigma y)^2/N)$$

where b' is the transpose of the vector b (the regression coefficients), X' is the transpose of the matrix X (the column of 1's for the intercept and the columns of dependent variables), and $((\Sigma y)^2/N)$ is the correction term used to arrive at deviation scores.

Line 41 creates vector bp (for "b prime") by taking the transpose of vector b. Line 42 creates matrix $bpxpy$ by multiplying vector bp and matrix xpy. Line 43 computes the sum of the values for y by applying the csum (column sum) function to matrix y. Line 44 squares this result, and line 45 divides that value by N (by applying the nrow [number of rows] function to matrix y). Line 46 creates a matrix called yp by taking the transpose of matrix y, and line 47 multiplies matrix yp and matrix y. Line 48 computes the regression sum of squares. Line 49 computes the residual sum of squares from the formula:

$$e'e = Y'Y - b'X'Y$$

where e' is a row vector of residuals and e is a column vector of residuals. Line 50 computes the total sum of squares by adding sum of squares regression and sum of squares residual.

```
51) *
52) * Compute R square
53) *.
54) compute rsq = ssreg/sstot.
```

Line 54 computes R^2, which represents the proportion of variance in the criterion (academic ability) accounted for by the predictor (parents' education), that is, the proportion of the total sum of squares accounted for by the regression sum of squares.

```
55) *
56) * Compute standard error of the estimate and F
57) *.
58) compute dfreg = ncol(x) - 1.
59) compute dfres = nrow(y) - dfreg - 1.
60) compute sterrest = sqrt(ssres/dfres).
61) compute f = (ssreg/dfreg)/(ssres/dfres).
```

These lines compute the required degrees of freedom so that the overall F test of significance can be computed. The regression degrees of freedom is the same as the number of predictors and is obtained in the first line by counting the number of columns (ncol function) in the matrix x and subtracting 1 (because there is a column of 1's for the intercept) (line 58). The residual degrees of freedom is obtained in line 59. The standard error of the estimate, which is the standard deviation of the residuals, is computed in line 60. Line 61 computes the F test for the overall model.

```
62) *
63) Compute standard error of coefficients and t values
64) *.
65) compute c = (ssres/dfres) * xpxinv.
66) compute cdiag = diag(c).
67) compute seb = sqrt(cdiag).
68) compute tval = b/seb.
```

Finally, we compute the standard errors of the regression coefficients and their associated t values. Line 65 creates a matrix called c that is the variance/covariance matrix of the regression coefficients from the formula:

$$c = (e'e/N - dfreg - 1)(X'X)^{-1}$$

For our present purpose, we are interested in the diagonal of c, because it contains the variance of the regression coefficients (i.e., the first element of the diagonal contains the variance for the first regression coefficient, the second element of the diagonal contains the variance for the second regression coefficient, and so forth). Line 66 creates a vector called *cdiag*, which contains the diagonal elements of matrix c by using the diag matrix function. Line 67 computes the standard errors for the coefficients using the sqrt matrix function, and line 68 computes the t values associated with the coefficients.

```
69) *
70) * Print results
71) *.
72) print rsq
73)    /title = 'R square (rsq).'
74) print sterrest
```

```
75)    /title = 'Standard error of the estimate (sterrest).'
76) print ssreg
77)    /title = 'Sum of squares regression (ssreg).'
78) print ssres
79)    /title = 'Sum of squares residual (ssres).'
80) print sstot
81)    /title = 'Sum of squares total (sstot).'
82) print f
83)    /title = 'F (f).'
84) print b
85)    /title = 'Regression coefficients (b).'
86) print seb
87)    /title = 'Standard errors of the regression coefficients (seb).'
88) print tval
89)    /title = 't values (tval).'
90) *
91) * End matrix processing
92) *.
93) end matrix.
```

Lines 72–89 instruct SPSS to print the results in the Output window so they may be seen. The end matrix command in line 93 concludes the matrix processing. Go ahead and enter these lines of code into the Syntax window and then run them. You will see the results shown in Figure 9.3, which you can compare with those provided in Figure 9.2 at the beginning of the chapter.

This example provides an opportunity to gain a fundamental understanding of SPSS matrix processing. You can expand your knowledge of the matrix language by consulting the SPSS syntax reference manual. I invite you to further reveal the power of this method by applying it to the more complicated tasks you may have at hand.

```
Run MATRIX procedure:

R square (rsq)
   .6290757032

Standard error of the estimate (sterrest)
   10.71733131

Sum of squares regression (ssreg)
   9350.442856

Sum of squares residual (ssres)
   5513.337144

Sum of squares total (sstot)
   10 ** 4    X
   1.486378000

F (f)
   81.40645953

Regression coefficients (b)
   1.658555174
   5.044967064

Standard errors of the regression
coefficients (seb)
   7.874700700
    .559150737

t values (tval)
    .210618186
   9.022552828


------ END MATRIX -----
```

Figure 9.3 Output From Second Example Matrix Procedure

EXERCISE FOURTEEN

Write a program using the SPSS matrix command language that demonstrates that the order of matrix multiplication makes a difference in the result. Comment each section of the program. Use the compute command and braces ({}) to write matrices A and B explicitly:

```
compute a = {1,2,3;4,5,6;7,8,9}.
compute b = {11,12,13;14,15,16;17,18,19}.
```

Multiply A times B and then multiply B times A. Print the results.

CHAPTER 10

Conclusion

This book covered a wide variety of intermediate and advanced skills for using the Statistical Package for the Social Sciences (SPSS) program. Having worked through this book, you have gained access to many of SPSS's exciting and powerful data analysis capabilities. Your SPSS skills have been considerably enhanced.

We have covered topics related to data files, looping functions, the SPSS macro facility, pivot tables, interactive graphics, the production facility, scripting, and the SPSS matrix command language. This book provided you with an introduction to these topics, and you are now capable of pursuing them further. I encourage you to do three things to further your skills:

❍ First, apply what you have learned in this book in as many different ways as you can think of in your own data analysis tasks.

❍ Second, remember that the SPSS manuals and the SPSS Web site contain a wealth of information; devote some time to finding additional information in them.

❍ Third, work with your colleagues to find even more ways to enhance and apply these skills.

Finally, as I mentioned at the beginning of this book, I encourage you to have fun as you apply SPSS to your research endeavors.

References

Einspruch, E. L. (1998). *An introductory guide to SPSS® for Windows®*. Thousand Oaks, CA: Sage Publications.

Iverson, G. R., & Norpoth, H. (1987). *Analysis of variance*. Thousand Oaks, CA: Sage Publications.

Lewis-Beck, M. S. (1995). *Data analysis: An introduction*. Thousand Oaks, CA: Sage Publications.

SPSS, Inc. (1999). *SPSS® Interactive Graphics 10.0*. Chicago, IL: Author.

SPSS, Inc. (1999). *SPSS® 10.0 Syntax Reference Guide*. Chicago, IL: Author.

SPSS, Inc. (2000). *SPSS® 10.0 Developer's Guide*. Chicago, IL: Author.

Solutions to Exercises

Exercise 1

```
*
* This code
*    Reads data from Norpoth (1987)
*    Documents the data file
*    Assigns variable and value labels
*    Displays the document
*    Lists cases
*    Conducts an ANOVA
*.
* Read the data.
file type nested file = "c: \norpoth87.txt" rec = #type 1 (a).
record type 'G'.
data list /
  type 2 tone 3.
record type 'S'.
data list /
  subject 2-3 score 4-5.
end file type.
* Document the data file.
document Example from Iverson and Norpoth (1987) in which
subjects in four groups watched a newscast about
economic issues and then rated the importance of
the economy as an issue.
* Assign variable and value labels.
variable labels
  type  'Type of story'/
  tone  'Tone of story'/
```

```
    score 'Subject rating of the importance of the economy as an issue.'
value labels
    type 1 'Unemployment'
         2 'Inflation'/
    tone 1 'Positive'
         2 'Negative.'

* Display the document.
display documents.
* List cases.
list cases/
    variables = all.
* Conduct ANOVA.
anova variables = score by type (1,2) tone (1,2).
```

ANOVA[a,b]

			Unique Method				
			Sum of Squares	df	Mean Square	F	Sig.
SCORE Subject rating of the importance of the economy as an issue	Main Effects	(Combined)	60.000	2	30.00	20.0	.001
		TYPE Type of story	12.000	1	12.00	8.00	.022
		TONE Tone of story	48.000	1	48.00	32.0	.000
	2-Way Interactions	TYPE Type of Story * TONE Tone of story	12.000	1	12.00	8.00	.022
	Model		72.000	3	24.00	16.0	.001
	Residual		12.000	8	1.500		
	Total		84.000	11	7.636		

a. SCORE Subject rating of the importance of the economy as an issue by TYPE Type of story, TONE Tone of story
b. All effects entered simultaneously

Exercise 2

```
* This code
*     Reads data from Norpoth (1987) in grouped format
*     Documents the data file
*     Autorecodes two variables
*     Assigns variable and value labels
*     Displays the document
*     Lists cases
*     Conducts an ANOVA
*     Saves the file
*     Clears the working data file

*     Displays the file information

*.
* Read the data.
file type grouped file = 'c:norpoth87b.txt'
  rec = #rec 3 case = subject 1-2.
record type 1.
data list/
  type 4 (a) tone 5 (a).
record type 2.
data list/
score 4-5.
end file type.
* Document the data file.
document Example from Iverson and Norpoth (1987) in which
subjects in four groups watched a newscast about
economic issues and then rated the importance of
the economy as an issue.
* Autorecode type and tone.
autorecode variables = type tone/
  into rtype rtone.
* Assign variable and value labels.
variable labels
  rtype   'Type of story'/
  rtone   'Tone of story'/
  score   'Subject rating of the importance of the economy as an issue.'
value labels
  rtype 1 'Unemployment'
        2 'Inflation'/
  rtone 1 'Positive'
        2 'Negative.'
```

```
* Display the document.
display documents.
* List cases.
list cases/
  variables = all.
* Conduct ANOVA.
anova variables = score by rtype (1,2) rtone (1,2).
* Save file.
save outfile = 'c:\norpoth87b.sav.'
* Clear working data file.

* new file.

* Display file information.

sysfile info file = 'c:\norpoth87b.sav'.
```

Exercise 3

First, type the following code in the SPSS syntax window and save it as "ExerciseThreeFileB.sps."

```
do if form = 'A'.
reread.
data list/
  subject 1-2 form 3 (a) type 4 tone 5 score 6-7.
end case.
else if form = 'B'.
reread.
data list/
  subject 1-2 form 3 (a) tone 4 type 5 score 6-7.
end case.
end if.
```

Next, clear the SPSS syntax window, type the following input program, save the program as "ExerciseThreeInput.sps," and run the program.

```
input program.
data list file = 'c:\ norpoth87c.txt' notable/
    form 3 (a).
```

```
include 'c:\ ExerciseThreeFileB.sps'.
end input program.
save outfile = 'c:\eric\nextstep\norpoth87c.sav'.
list cases.
```

ANSWER APPENDIX

Exercise 4

```
*
* This code
*    Reads data from Norpoth (1987)
*    Assigns variable and value labels
*    Lists cases
*    Writes a keyword macro to conduct an ANOVA
*    Calls the macro
*.
* Read the data.
file type nested file = "c:\norpoth87.txt" rec= #type 1 (a).
record type 'G'.
data list /
  type 2 tone 3.
record type 'S'.
data list /
  subject 2-3 score 4-5.
end file type.
* Assign variable and value labels.
variable labels
  type   'Type of story'/
  tone   'Tone of story'/
  score 'Subject rating of the importance of the economy as an issue.'
value labels
  type 1 'Unemployment'
       2 'Inflation'/
  tone 1 'Positive'
       2 'Negative'.
* List cases.
list cases/
  variables = all.
* Write macro to conduct ANOVA.
define noranova (depvar = !tokens(1)/
                 factor1 = !tokens(6)/
                 factor2 = !tokens(6)).
```

```
anova variables = !depvar by !factor1 !factor2.
!enddefine.
* Call macro to conduct ANOVA.
noranova depvar = score factor1 = type (1,2) factor2 = tone (1,2).
```

Exercise 5

```
*
* This code
*    Reads data from Norpoth (1987)
*    Assigns variable and value labels
*    Lists cases
*    Writes a positional macro to conduct an ANOVA
*    Calls the macro
*.
* Read the data.
file type nested file = "c:\norpoth87.txt" rec= #type 1 (a).
record type 'G'.
data list /
  type 2 tone 3.
record type 'S'.
data list /
   subject 2-3 score 4-5.
end file type.
* Assign variable and value labels.
variable labels
  type  'Type of story'/
  tone  'Tone of story'/
  score 'Subject rating of the importance of the economy as an issue.'
value labels
  type 1 'Unemployment'
       2 'Inflation'/
  tone 1 'Positive'
       2 'Negative'.
* List cases.
list cases/
   variables = all.
* Write macro to conduct ANOVA.
define noranova (!positional !tokens(1)/
                 !positional !tokens(6)/
                 !positional !tokens(6)).
```

G Gender * AE Advisor Evaluation Cross Tabulation

| | | AE Advisor Evaluation | | | | | | | | |
| | | .00 Fail | | 1.00 Succeed or Fail | | 2.00 Succeed | | Total | |
		Count	% within G Gender	Count	% within G Gender	Count	% within G Gender	Count	% within G Gender
G Gender	.00 Male	7	25.0%	14	50.0%	7	25.0%	28	100.0%
	1.00 Female	6	27.3%	11	50.0%	5	22.7%	22	100.0%
Total		13	26.0%	25	50.0%	12	24.0%	50	100.0%

Advisor evaluations were similar for males and females.

Figure A.1 Pivot Table After Operations in Exercise 6 Have Been Applied

```
anova variables = !1 by !2 !3.
!enddefine.
* Call macro to conduct ANOVA.
noranova score type (1,2) tone (1,2).
```

Exercise 6

Work through each of the steps in the exercise. The resulting pivot table should look like Figure A.1.

Exercise 7

Your chart will look like Figure A.2.

Go ahead and rerun the chart, selecting different options, to see how the Interactive Charts feature can dynamically allow you to change how the results appear.

Exercise 8

First, open the Wintergreen data set, from the pull-down menus select **Analyze, Compare Means, Means** . . . , select "pe" for the dependent variable and "g" for the independent variable, and click the "Continue"

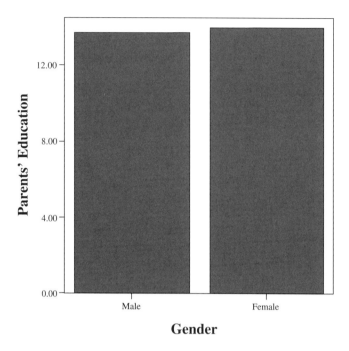

Gender

Figure A.2 Output From Interactive Chart

button, click the "OK" button. Then, double-click the pivot table to activate it, select the two mean values (13.7143 and 13.9545), and right-click within the selected area and choose **Create Graph, Bar.** Your graph will be similar to the one you created for Exercise 7. You may use the Chart Manager to alter the appearance of the graph if you wish.

Exercise 9

Your production facility dialog box will look like that in Figure A.3, except that your files may be stored in different folders.

The output from your production job should match your output from Exercise 1.

Exercise 10

Change the line in the syntax file that reads

```
anova variables = score by type (1,2) tone (1,2).
```

to read

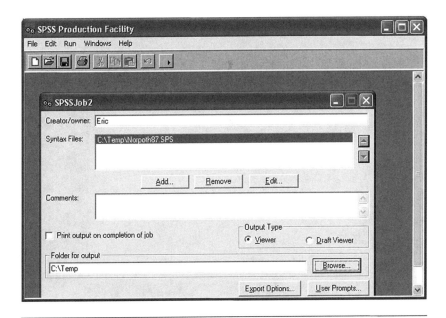

Figure A.3 Production Facility Dialog Box After Operations in Exercise 9 Have Been Applied

```
anova variables = @depvar by @factor1 @factor2
```

Your production job dialog box will look like Figure A.4 (of course your files may be in a different location and your comments may be different).

Your user prompts dialog box will look like Figure A.5.

View the output and confirm it matches the output obtained in Exercise 1.

Exercise 11

Select the ANOVA table in the output by single-clicking it (if you double-click it, you will activate the table rather than selecting). The script is called "Make totals bold.sbs" and may be found in the " . . . \spss\scripts" folder. As its name states, the script makes the "Total" line in the table bold, as shown in Figure A.6.

Exercise 12

To open the Script window, select **File, New, Script** from the pull-down menus. The script is called "Make totals bold.sbs" and resides in

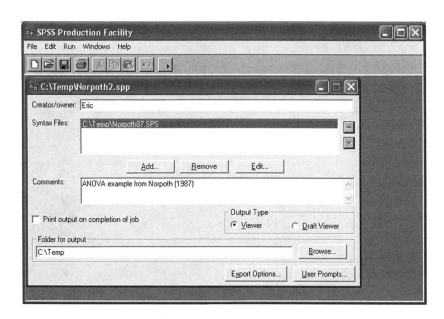

Figure A.4 Production Facility Dialog Box After Operations in Exercise 10 Have Been Applied

the "\spss\scripts" folder. Double-click the file to open it in the Script Editor window. Change the two lines that read

```
.TextStyle = 2 'Bold text'
'.TextStyle' = 3 'Bold Italic text'
```

to

```
'.TextStyle' = 2 'Bold text'
.TextStyle = 3  'Bold Italic text'
```

Change the two lines of code that read

```
'.TextColor' = RGB(255, 0, 0)                'Red'
.TextColor  = RGB(0, 0, 255)                'Blue'
```

to

```
.TextColor  = RGB(255, 0, 0)                'Red'
'.TextColor' = RGB(0, 0, 255)                'Blue'
```

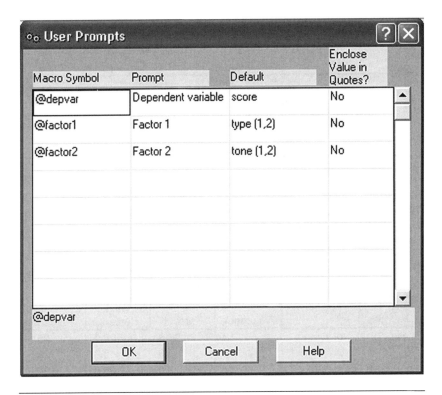

Figure A.5 User Prompts Dialog Box After Operations in Exercise 10 Have Been Applied

ANOVA[a,b]

			Unique Method				
			Sum of Squares	df	Mean Square	F	Sig.
SCORE	Main Effects	(Combined)	60.000	2	30.000	20.000	.001
		TYPE	12.000	1	12.000	8.000	.022
		TONE	48.000	1	48.000	32.000	.000
	2-Way Interactions	TYPE * TONE	12.000	1	12.000	8.000	.022
	Model		72.000	3	24.000	16.000	.001
	Residual		12.000	8	1.500		
	Total		84.000	11	7.636		

a. SCORE by TYPE, TONE

b. All effects entered simultaneously

Figure A.6 ANOVA Table After Running Script to Make Totals Bold

ANOVA[a,b]

			Unique Method				
			Sum of Squares	df	Mean Square	F	Sig.
SCORE	Main Effects	(Combined)	60.000	2	30.000	20.000	.001
		TYPE	12.000	1	12.000	8.000	.022
		TONE	48.000	1	48.000	32.000	.000
	2-Way Interactions	TYPE * TONE	12.000	1	12.000	8.000	.022
	Model		72.000	3	24.000	16.000	.001
	Residual		12.000	8	1.500		
	Total		84.000	11	7.636		

a. SCORE by TYPE, TONE
b. All effects entered simultaneously

Figure A.7 ANOVA Table After Running Script to Make Totals Bold, Italic, and Red

SM Student Motivation

		Frequency	Percent	Valid Percent	Cumulative Percent
Valid	.00 Not Willing	13	26.0	26.0	26.0
	1.00 Undecided	23	46.0	46.0	72.0
	2.00 Willing	14	28.0	28.0	100.0
	Total	50	100.0	100.0	

Figure A.8 Frequency Distribution of Student Motivation

Save the script as 'MakeTotalsBoldItalicRed.' Select the ANOVA table and run the script. The "Total" line in the table is now bold italic and red rather than bold and blue, as shown in Figure A.7.

Exercise 13

Open the Wintergreen data set and run a frequency distribution on the variable "student motivation." The output table looks like that in Figure A.8.

Single-click on the table to select it. From the pull-down menus select **Edit, Options . . . .** The options dialog box appears. Select the "Scripts" tab. Check the box next to the autoscript titled "Frequencies_Table_Frequencies_Create." Click the "OK" button and rerun the frequency

SM Student Motivation

		Frequency	Percent	Valid Percent	Cumulative Percent
Valid	.00 Not Willing	13	26.0	26.0	26.0
	1.00 Undecided	23	46.0	46.0	72.0
	2.00 Willing	14	28.0	28.0	100.0
	Total	**50**	**100.0**	**100.0**	

Figure A.9 Frequency Distribution of Student Motivation With Autoscript Enabled

distribution. The output table now looks like that in Figure A.9 (notice that the last "Total" row has been made bold).

Exercise 14

The syntax file contains these lines of code:

```
*
* Clear the working data file
*.

new file.

*
* Start matrix processing
*.

matrix.

*
* Compute matrices a and b explicitly
*.

compute a = {1,2,3;4,5,6;7,8,9}.

compute b = {11,12,13;14,15,16;17,18,19}.

*
* Multiply a times b
```

```
*.

compute ab = a * b.

*
* Multiply b times a
*.

compute ba = b * a.

*
* Print results
*.

print a
  / title = 'Matrix A.'
print b
  / title = 'Matrix B.'
print ab
  / title = 'Matrix AB.'
print ba
  / title = 'Matrix BA.'

*
* End matrix processing
*.

end matrix.
```

The output looks like that in Figure A.10.

```
Run MATRIX procedure:

Matrix A
    1   2   3
    4   5   6
    7   8   9

Matrix B
   11   12   13
   14   15   16
   17   18   19

Matrix AB
    90    96   102
   216   231   246
   342   366   390

Matrix BA
   150   186   222
   186   231   276
   222   276   330


------  END MATRIX  -----
```

Figure A.10   Matrix Procedure Output From Exercise 14

Index

About the Author

Eric L. Einspruch is a Senior Research Associate at RMC Research Corporation in Portland, Oregon. He received his BA from The Evergreen State College in Olympia, Washington, and he received his MSEd in counseling psychology and his PhD in educational research and evaluation from the University of Miami in Coral Gables, Florida. Much of his experience with large-scale data analysis was gained working in the Office of Institutional Research at Miami-Dade Community College. He has taught courses in statistical methods and in computer applications in educational research. He is currently involved in the evaluation of school-based and community-based social service programs and in large-scale surveys. His publications have appeared in the *Florida Journal of Educational Research, International Journal of Early Childhood, Psychotherapy in Private Practice, Journal of Drug Education, Journal of Counseling Psychology, Journal of Primary Prevention,* and *Reaching Today's Youth.*